ISBN 978-09560699-48

Published July 2012 by
Coolcanals Guides
Suite 131, 79 Friar Street
Worcester, Worcestershire
WR1 2NT
info@coolcanals.com
www.coolcanals.com

Jacket design by Craig Stevens,
www.craig-stevens.co.uk
Jacket images by coolcanals

OUR THANKS
A huge thanks to those who kindly
contributed - we are honoured and deeply
grateful to: Julia Bradbury, Paul Atterbury,
Tony Hales, John Bridgeman, Peter Collins,
Ian McMillan, and Nigel Crowe.

Very special thanks to everyone from the
Canal & River Trust who have so generously
given their time and expertise, especially:
Ed Fox, Nayna Tarver, John Bridgeman,
Linda Barley, Hannah Kitchener.

Thanks also to those who have absolutely
nothing to do with the making of this
guidebook, but who help to keep Britain's
waterways open for everyone to enjoy.

Big thanks to DiGi-Masters.com, the techies
behind our website - www.coolcanals.com

And hugs to rescue dogs Lenny the lurcher
and Meg the marvellous mongrel who've
visited the coolcanals boat to keep us
cheerful since Tufty our last boat cat sadly
passed away.

PHOTO CREDITS
Martine's photos are taken along our
travels. We thank any canal folk, and their
boats, who are framed in our pics.

All photographs © Martine O'Callaghan
www.coolcanals.com

Apart from the following, reproduced
with much thanks by kind permission of:

© Canal & River Trust p7 (J Bridgeman, N
Crowe & T Hales), p138, p139, p185, p216;
© Waterways Archive / Waterways Trust
p11, p12, p25, p31, p59, p62, p63, p113,
p120, p121, p133, p158, p162, p207, p223;
© Paul Atterbury p38, p39;
© John Bridgeman Collection p188;
© Antony Dunn p16;
© Nick Holt p7 (J Bradbury), p110;
© George Lloyd p85;
© London Canal Museum p106, p107;
© Adrian Mealing p7 (I McMillan);
© Chris Turner at Enjoy Photography p49;

OUR ETHICS & THE ENVIRONMENT
We aim to inspire visitors to enjoy
Britain's canals, and help protect its
living heritage, nature and wildlife. We
hope that, in our own small way, we are
supporting the community, culture and
traditions that make our canals so special.

Because we care about the whole earth
as well as the waterways, we 'think'
green throughout every part of the
process of making our guides: from
running Coolcanals in our eco narrowboat
office, to choosing eco award-winning
UK printers.

Printed and bound in the UK by
Butler Tanner & Dennis, Frome,
Somerset.

'Britain's canals, a national treasure in
100 must-see objects' is printed using
100% vegetable-based inks on paper that
has a Forest Stewardship Council (FSC)
certification. All FSC-certified papers are
produced by companies who support
well-managed forestry schemes which in
turn actively plant and replace trees that
are cut down for pulp, typically planting
more trees than are harvested. Butler
Tanner and Dennis are also fully ISO14001
accredited and, by both printing and
binding on one site, dramatically reduce
their impact on the environment.

BRITAIN'S

A national treasure in 100 *must-see* objects

CANALS

Phillippa Greenwood & Martine O'Callaghan

Contents

100 treasures to discover
all across the canals of Britain...
exploring over 2,000 miles

Introduction to this book

coolcanals - Phillippa & Martine
Britain's canals have taken us to all sorts of extremes. We're incurably prolific towpath trekkers, ambling and rambling the canals all across Britain from the sands of Cornwall to the Highlands of Scotland - and we live on a narrowboat too. Our passion for canals unashamedly fills our books with inspiration we like to share.

This book is a celebration of the canals of England, Scotland and Wales, spanning over 2,000 miles and 200 years of British heritage – a national treasure.

Canals mean something different to everyone. Some come for space to think, or to be alone with the dog, others love the activity of boating, walking or cycling, while some just like to sightsee. Canals are a parallel world, as different as any faraway place, and towpath tourists come to wonder at the architecture, marvels of engineering, the intrigue of canal museums, and enjoy the living heritage that makes Britain's canals so special today.

Each of the 100 'objects' is a canal treasure that can be seen, or tangibly experienced. Not all treasures are made of gold - some speak only of the wonders of simplicity that make Britain's canals uniquely idyllic.

Everyone has their favourite treasure of the canals and picking only 100 was always going to be an impossible task. We've chosen some of the best treasures that tell the story of the canals past, present and future, and why people come here - and we've asked some experts who love the canals to choose their favourites too. Some of the 100 are heritage marvels that no canal book should miss, others are honeypot sites of modern leisure and tourism, and then there are the little things that burn into your soul and create the life of the canals - hedgerows, swans, the sounds of ducks at dawn.

It's a national pastime to visit places of historic interest, but we didn't want to write a history book that would creak and groan, since that wouldn't represent the life of the canals we know and love today. Canals were built over 200 years ago, yet refuse to grow old. A historic transport route has reinvented itself as a leisure destination and canals are cool again. This book aims to illuminate the living heritage of Britain's canals, and inspire you to visit as often as you can, escape the hurried world and steep yourself in the many treasures of the waterways.

The 100 collectively act as keepers of the diverse story of our canals. But of course the story is ongoing, and more and more people are discovering their own treasures every day across the canals. So this book is just the beginning - share your favourite treasure of the canals on our website... and join in telling the story of Britain's canals. The genuine passion people feel for canals is one of the most precious wonders of the waterways.

Enjoy!

Phillippa & Martine

Your favourite canal treasure
Join in telling the story - visit our website www.coolcanals.com/100treasures and share your favourite treasure of the canals

And thanks to our contributors for choosing their favourites

'Treasure' 12 - Paul Atterbury:
Art historian, writer, transport enthusiast and expert on BBC Television's Antiques Roadshow, vice president of the Waterways Trust (now merged with British Waterways into the Canal & River Trust), and rumoured to be the inspiration for the famous 'Watch With Mother' puppet Andy Pandy, whose strings were pulled by his mother.

'Treasure' 48 - Julia Bradbury:
TV Presenter, Ramblers Vice-President and walking personality. She's always busy - since exploring four great canals in her 'Canal Walks' series for BBC, she's become a mother to Zeph, mingled with wild bears in the woods of Minnesota for 'Planet Earth Live' and won 'People's Campaigner' in the 2012 National Trust Octavia Hill Awards. www.juliabradbury.com

'Treasures' 9, 54, 86 - John Bridgeman CBE TD DL:
Vice Chairman of British Waterways and Trustee of the Canal & River Trust. Born and educated in Wales, John has had a lifetime interest in the Glamorganshire Canal and has supported and helped raise funds for the Montgomery Canal, Heritage Boatyard at Ellesmere Port and Wilts & Berks Canal Society. He is a Deputy Lord Lieutenant, Honorary Colonel of the Queen's Own Oxfordshire Hussars and Trustee of a number of charities.

'Treasure' 73 - Peter Collins:
Collections Manager at the National Waterways Museum

'Treasures' 15, 21, 25, 36, 47, 50, 60, 65, 77, 80, 83 ,93, 98 -
Nigel Crowe:
Head of Heritage for the Canal & River Trust

'Treasure' 27 - Tony Hales CBE:
Chairman of the Canal & River Trust. Tony is a longtime supporter of Britain's waterways and a virtual treasure of the canals himself!

'Treasure' 1 - Ian McMillan:
Poet, comedian & broadcaster, Ian hosts weekly radio show The Verb for BBC, and is a regular on programmes such as Coast, Pick of the Week and The Arts Show. A life-long supporter of Barnsley FC, he is the club's Poet-in-Residence. He is a Vice President of the Poetry Society.
www.poetrysociety.org.uk

Introduction to the canals

Something mellow rumbles deeply in our emotions when we step onto a canal towpath...

Canals stride all across Britain, secretly holding the story of an empire and a thrilling tale of two centuries. Yet with never a dull moment in their history, the canals are far more than just living heritage - they are a treasure of today and a beacon for the future.

There are over 2,000 miles of inland waterways scrambling from the wild Highlands of Scotland to the sands of Cornwall, touching the Pennines, the Dales, the Peak District, Brecon Beacons, Birmingham, Stratford-upon-Avon, Bath, London and almost everywhere in between. Canals link city to city, valleys to mountains, docks to factories, and beaches to the furthest reaches inland. The wonder of these waterways is that their idyllic tranquillity scarcely betrays itself as they bulldog through the contours of Britain with unfathomable lock flights, amazing aqueducts and fiercely dark tunnels.

Canals hobnob with the Pyramids, the Acropolis, the Great Wall of China, with their own World Heritage sites such as Pontcysyllte Aqueduct and Saltaire. And every way Britain turns, it can't help but revel in the simplicity of canals too. A toddler feeding the ducks, a weathered boater teaching the ropes, walkers with dogs, families on bikes... The notorious camaraderie of canal life has evolved through the people who've lived and worked here, and now those who visit for leisure. Travel defines its community, nurtures camaraderie, and cherishes old-fashioned ways that let strangers nod as they pass by.

The beautiful irony is that canals that were built for speed as the 4mph transport routes of the Industrial Revolution, have now become a haven for people and wildlife to escape the urbanism and materialism that the canals once helped to create.

The rush of modern living loses its bearings in the tranquil world of canals, where the water's slow mantra beats with the rhythms of nature and the fastest speed is set by a duckling chasing its mum. The inland waterways have become the nation's new leisure destination, yet with over 2,000 miles of water road, it's easy to escape the crowds and relax in rural solitude. Antidotes to stress come with the clinking of mooring rings, the hoot of an invisible moorhen, the occasional splosh of a heron fishing and the chilled put-put of approaching narrowboats. Whether you holiday in a boat or just take a stroll along a towpath, it's impossible not to be drawn into the spirit of the canals. It's the car-free slow destination waiting to be explored: a place to chill out, do something different, a haven away from it all, a national treasure.

The History of Canals (in a nutshell)

Man has battled to master his environment since time began, and manmade water routes have played a leading role in the history of the world. It is thought that the **first canal** was built in **Mesopotamia** in **4000BC** to improve navigation on impossibly slow rivers. In the 6th century, the great emperors of China were early canal builders, and they used a network of managed water routes to control their empire. The **Grand Canal in China** was started in 540 and throughout its alarming construction 5 million labourers worked on it, and 2 million died of exhaustion or accidents. The canal eventually linked the Yellow River to the Yangtse in an incredible 1,000-mile route that is still in use today. Venice is perhaps the most vocal canal city in the world, immortalised in the paintings of Titian, Canaletto and all the masters of those fabulous frescoes. The city was founded in the 5th century and became a mighty trading place at its peak in the 15th century. The **Romans** also grasped the power of canals and brought their canal schemes to Britain in AD65 as they dug the **Fossdyke**.

Britain, like any island that has water running through its history, can only write its complete story through the waves that flow full circle around its coast. Since time began, rivers and seas have worked in partnership with invaders and defenders, and Britain once sailed the seas to 'discover' new worlds. From the king's forests, great oaks made mighty royal ships that set off arrogantly and adventurously to conquer the world and bring back rum, spices and stories. **Seas** and bold ships once drove the British Empire and, at its most flamboyant, the coast hails centuries-old stories of white-water conquests; yet **canals and rivers** that quietly tiptoed inland, reached into the heart of an island, and laid the deepest secrets that still humbly hide some of the nation's best **treasures**.

In times of great adventurers, **trade routes** romantically scurried the globe from sea to sea and then inland from our shores by water routes. The importance of a city was once the size of its **river**. London had the Thames, Liverpool the Mersey and Bristol the Avon. But the **arrival of the canals** and the **Industrial Revolution** created a new urban geography that **changed the map**. Factories erupted on the skyline wherever canals could link with raw materials and markets. **Birmingham** became England's second city, and the capital of the canals.

Britain's canal system was born from a fabulous inferno of wild **entrepreneurism** and all the bravado of British **engineering** ingenuity. **Navvies** arrived with shovels, to be told by the canal companies to dig 'the cut' that would change the world. Over 200 years later we can look back at an innovative network of trade routes that were built on the arrogance, and brilliance, of the Industrial Revolution.

The period in British history known as **'Canal Mania'** (1790s-1810s) was a time of unprecedented **change**. Businessmen were crazed with the possibilities of growth, while the greatest engineers couldn't work fast enough to keep up. It's even thought that overwork killed James Brindley, the pioneering canal engineer who built the first canal in England, the Bridgwater Canal (1761). Canal Mania saw up to **20 new canals** approved by parliament in one year - shockingly comparable to 20 new motorways scaring the countryside all in one year today, or 20 HS2 (High Speed 2) train tracks causing uproar in leafy suburbia.

In the mad dig, chaos swiped the countryside and when navvies turned up with their hard skin and rough ways, local villagers were often afraid of the invasion. The soft apartheid between the canal world and the rest of Britain was already set. Rich landowners didn't always welcome the scar on their estates and made the same arguments as landowners today when threatened by a new transport route cutting through their doorstep. Many sights on the canals today tell the story of how canal plans had to compromise with the demands of landowners - such as Tixall Wide on the Staffordshire & Worcestershire Canal where landowner Thomas Clifford forced a section of canal to be widened to create the illusion that the trade route cutting into his viewpoint was a pretty lake.

Canals were built to function as **a new national transport system**. They had to connect industry, raw materials, ports and markets in a network of manmade water routes, taking boats where nature never intended them to go. They carved trade routes for salt, coal, iron, pottery, textiles and more. During the Industrial Revolution, these vital trade routes allowed Britain's manufacturing business to dominate the world... And canals carried the 'Made in Britain' label to its highest peak.

The new **factories** of the mass manufacturing era needed labourers, and that led to the **migration** of people. Agricultural workers who belonged in Haywain landscapes were forced by poverty to climb into barges that would take them to new employment in the **industrial towns** of the Midlands and the North. Sadly, the brave new urbanism had its dark side, with Dickensian stories unfolding. Entrepreneurs seized every opportunity that champed in the boom years, yet injustices of poverty often became the trials of life for the urban masses. Harsh as their lives were, nothing compared to the misery African people were suffering under the hat of 'slavery'. Much of the British manufacturing business profited from unfair trade and slave labour in the cotton fields and sugar plantations of the Americas. Quaker dynasties and other philanthropic powers that led many of the most successful businesses of the canal era joined the Africans in their rebellion, and by the late 18th century abolitionists were campaigning with force. Josiah Wedgwood used his pottery as a tool for dissent as he produced an anti-slavery medallion with the portrait of a kneeling African man shackled in chains - 'Am I not a man and a brother?' His medallion was picked up as a sort of 'logo' for the fight against slavery.

As canals around the world got bigger, and more ambitious, slave trade routes were diluted by other options for trade. The Suez Canal opened in 1869 for full-sized ships and its short cut reduced the voyage from Britain to India from 10,800 miles to 6,300 miles. For the first time cotton fibre from India could challenge American cotton. Wedgwood pushed Britain to seize the opportunity in the sugar industries too, and he had special sugar bowls made in his factory with inscriptions promoting sugar grown in East India as opposed to sugar from the plantations in the West Indies.

Britain earned the nickname '**workshop of the world**' as its manufacturing industries grafted across its green and pleasant land in the cause of mass production. Working narrowboats could scarcely carry enough cargo, or transport goods fast enough. The earliest narrowboats were

pulled by horses, donkeys or mules. But when the giddy excitement of the steam engine arrived, the waterways dived into a new era with monster horse power. Then, and now, the honey-deep 'phwt-phwt-phwt' rhythm of a traditional narrowboat engine gliding through water can turn men into boys, and women into men.

At first it was only the men who crewed the working narrowboats, but later, for economic reasons, their famiies joined them. Whole families lived aboard in the tiny **boatman's cabin**, and their homes were highly decorated with traditional canal art of roses and castles. Canal people had their own community, and lived segregated from wider society that often shunned them (just as they had not trusted the navvies who built the canals). Today, in a topsy-turvy twist, it's the same separation between two worlds that makes canal life so idyllically unique and very special.

The great exhibition in 1851 (held in the original Crystal Palace in London) was organised by Prince Albert in a display that unleashed the nation's overwhelming excitement and pride in British

Engineering. After Queen Victoria's visit to the exhibition, she reported in her diary, "...What used to be done by hand and used to take months doing is now accomplished in a few instants by the most beautiful machinery..." Her revelations over the aesthetics of function paint an uplifting picture of the marvellous achievements of the Victorian period, yet glossed over the sweaty plight of frustrated factory workers and unfair pay for women, and the growing number of movements setting out to challenge the new class structure that force fed prejudice.

The stenching noise and urban smog of the **manufacturing years** needed an antidote, and **trends in the arts** obliged. **Romanticism** was a movement in art, literature and music that flung aside the corsets of inhibition to express human feelings and commune with nature. William Wordsworth (1770-1850) was amongst the greatest thinkers of the time who fed the nation with spoonfuls of reaction from the reality of materialism - 'and it is my faith, that every flower enjoys the air it breathes'. His religious euphoria was rooted in nature, and every generation since has acknowledged 'a crowd of daffodils' as a ray of joy over Britain. John Keats (1795-1821) wrote, 'A thing of beauty is a joy forever', and William Blake's (1757-1827) work coiled his want for freedom of the imagination too. His famous words sing notoriously from 'Jerusalem' - 'And did those feet in ancient time/Walk upon England's mountains green'.

While the boys were raving about fields of flowers, the girls had their attention on love, and Jane Austen (1775-1817) was the guru of such matters. Her work turned a blind eye to the canals, even though she lived in Bath with a canal on her doorstep. And, similarly, Constable (1776-1837) preferred to paint the English Idyll in landscapes that avoided canals and the ugly industrial epidemic of his time. Ironically, for that same sentiment, Constable would probably hunt out canal towpaths to set up his easel if he was alive today.

Although canals are under-represented in the fine arts of the Canal Mania era, they do appear in the work of Turner (1775-1851), Ford Madox Brown (1821-1893) and others, and there is an explicit collection of drawings and paintings of Britain's canals that can be seen in the archive from the Great Exhibition of 1851 www.royalcommission1851.org.uk. So art has had its say, and recorded the history of canals for future generations to unravel. Many illuminating photos are kept in the collections of the National Waterways Archive at Ellesmere Port www.nwm.org.uk. Yet the story isn't over, art today reflects and feeds the changes of a waterways system that is constantly reinventing itself. Contemporary sculpture, conceptual art and installation art play with the modern moods of the water, and traditional canal artists such as Tony Lewery keep the true colours of the cut en vogue too.

Even the **English language** itself has been influenced by the era of industrialisation and Canal Mania. Great inventors such as James Watt (1736-1819) introduced words that have everyday meaning today - 'Watt' became a unit of power. And James Watt was the first to use the term

'horsepower' in a bid to explain a unit measure of the new engines that had arrived to take the place of horses towing boats. Terms such as 'icebreaker' date back to sturdy little boats that once thrust through frozen canals and rivers to clear the way for narrowboats and barges to fulfil a day's work. Phrases such as 'wouldn't touch it with a bargepole' have obvious connections, and if a person is said to be 'barging through', the lumbering perception is not unlike the image of those flat-bottomed travellers.

After the **railways arrived**, canals struggled to survive in changing times where haulage was no longer willing to travel at 4mph. The first public **steam locomotive** was operated by

George Stephenson in 1825, and by the 1840s the railway boom was in full flurry. By 1930 Britain had over 19,000 miles of rail tracks. Canal companies were being put out of business and many were doomed by neglect from an emerging motorway nation that no longer needed canals.

Progress left the Victorians wanting respite from the smog of their new urban lives, and so they invented the great **British holiday**. The 'factory fortnight' and 'Bank holidays' were going to stamp free time on the calendar, and since human nature is drawn to water, it made sense that an island's population would head for the coast. The railway era made the seaside accessible to the masses, bringing deckchairs and chip shops to swamp Britain's chosen beaches, and typical Victorian engineering poked piers into the ocean for seaside fun. Inevitably, no sensible Victorian would see a disused water-motorway as a desirable place for leisure - it was too soon, just as if we closed the M6 today.

The horror of the Nazi holocaust, and the real threat of Hitler invading Britain's homeland became the sad years of **World War II**. The canals could have been a useful mapping route for invading forces, so signposts and mileposts were removed (some survived and were replaced after the war). But the water road was an asset as a transport route for the Allied war effort too. While men were fighting on the front, women were called to work on canalboats carrying essential supplies and vital components for the famous Spitfire aeroplanes. The band of feisty women who volunteered for the task, all wore a badge with the initials IW (for Inland Waterways) - the initials led to the affectionate, if wholly inaccurate, nickname '**Idle Women**'.

Passions reared for the fate of lost canals in the post-war generation, with an uprising of small voices making a big noise to stamp the **restoration years**. In 1939 Tom Rolt took his narrowboat 'Cressy' on a legendary journey, cruising for pleasure, not haulage. His struggle to navigate neglected canals resulted in the foundation of the campaigning group now famously known as the **Inland Waterways Association**. The IWA gathered a voice through growing numbers of boaters who wanted to help protect the canals and keep them navigable for boats. Rolt, a quiet but visionary man, had unwittingly become the founding father of tourism on Britain's canals.

The waterways no longer depend on the manufacturing trades of the Industrial Revolution - today its main industry is **tourism**. With hindsight we can see that materialism had to be the prize and sacrifice of the Industrial Revolution. We measure national wealth by money and 'things', yet society and wellbeing are less quantifiable. We work hard and go shopping to anonymous malls for short-term gratification. But nature leaves us wanting respite: holidays, days out, time off. To **escape** from noise and distraction, we go to the waterways to find more satisfying stuff than money can buy. In an odd twist of fate, canals have become a retreat from the consumer mayhem they once helped create. In sleepiest green England, Wales and Scotland, tourists willingly flock to the inland waterways to **walk, cycle, sightsee, wildlife watch or go boating**. Even in unlikely parts of the Midlands and the North where mills and foundries once spewed over the skyline, relics of industry have transformed into **tourist attractions** of industrial heritage too.

Today, when historic **horse-pulled narrowboats** nostalgically re-enact bygone scenes, British tourism is showing its **pride** for the part canals played in making Britain 'Great'. Canals came before the motor engine, electricity, television and the internet... yet remarkably they have remained **unspoilt by progress**, unchanged in over two centuries, and still carry narrowboats uphill and downhill with unsurpassable, ingenious, jaw-dropping simplicity. How cool is that!

Find out more about the fascinating story of Britain's canals from our website www.coolcanals.com or visit the official website of the Canal & River Trust who care for canals today www.canalandrivertrust.org

WATERWAYS TIMELINE

BC

c. 4000BC
MESOPOTAMIA
manmade improvements to aid navigation on slow rivers

6th Century
GRAND CANAL IN CHINA

AD65
THE ROMANS Fossdyke

THE MIDDLE AGES
Estuarial rivers were used for transporting cargo

16th & 17th Century
NAVIGABLE RIVERS
River navigation improvements began with the Thames locks and the River Wey Navigation. The River Wey was one of the first canalised rivers in England, built by Sir Richard Weston 1635-1653, allowing navigable waters for barges to transport goods to London

1500s

1533-1603
QUEEN ELIZABETH I

1564-1616
WILLIAM SHAKESPEARE

1600s

Late 1700s / Early 1800s
CANAL MANIA - THE ERA OF CANAL BUILDING
The first fully manmade canal was the Bridgewater Canal, opened in 1761, and for the next half century the rivers Thames, Severn, Trent and Mersey were linked by narrow canals. At the height of Canal Mania, there were over 6,000 miles of navigable rivers and canals scrambling across Britain's landscape - connecting mines and other raw materials, to factories, mills, and ports

THE INDUSTRIAL REVOLUTION
Grips Britain & dominates world markets with mass production in new factories. The exciting era of great entrepreneurs and engineers as well as horrors of 'dark satanic mills'

Early 1800s
RAIL MANIA
The steam engine brings the arrival of the railways - making the slower canal systems old fashioned. Rail Mania took over and canals fell into commercial decline. 1829 George Stephenson's 'Rocket' made its first journey

1869
SUEZ CANAL

1700s

1728
CAPTAIN COOK
Born in Marton.
His famous ocean-going vessel was the Endeavour

Late 18th Century
LUNAR SOCIETY

1800s

1807
ABOLITION OF SLAVE TRADE

1815
BATTLE OF WATERLOO
Wellington victorious over Napoleon at Waterloo

1837
QUEEN VICTORIA
Came to the throne

1851
THE GREAT EXHIBITION
organised by Prince Albert

1885
MOTOR CAR invented
by Karl Benz

1914
PANAMA CANAL was completed and became the world's longest ship canal

1939-1945
IDLE WOMEN
Women joined up to do their bit for the war effort working on canal boats carrying essential supplies along the nation's waterways. The women wore badges with the initials of the Inland Waterways, IW, which is how they got the nickname 'Idle Women'

1946
IWA (Inland Waterways Association) formed by Tom Rolt and Richard Aickman

1948
BRITAIN'S CANALS NATIONALISED

1960s
CANAL CLOSURES
Canals fall into disrepair. Many are lost or become unnavigable

1962
BRITISH WATERWAYS BOARD formed
(later to become British Waterways)

Mid 1980s
BIRMINGHAM'S Brindley Place & LONDON'S docklands redeveloped

THE RESTORATION YEARS
Volunteers and organisations work together... building, campaigning, raising funds and protesting over DEFRA cuts

2000s
2nd CANAL MANIA
Tourism on the canals booms. Narrowboat builders struggle to keep supply with record demand. The mod-con revolution of new fully-fitted boats with central heating, TVs and gadgets attracts a new era of boaters

2012
NEW CHARITY STATUS
British Waterways become Canal & River Trust

April 1912
RMS TITANIC SANK

1914-1918
WORLD WAR I

Late 19th / early 20th century
SUFFRAGETTE MOVEMENT - 1918
Women over 30 won the right to vote

1929
FIRST TV BROADCAST by BBC

1939-1945
WORLD WAR II

1952
QUEEN ELIZABETH II
Came to the throne

1959
FIRST MOTORWAY
M1 opened

1980s-1990s
INTERNET REVOLUTION

2012
QUEEN ELIZABETH II
Diamond Jubilee

1 'CANAL LIFE'

A poem to mark the launch of the Canal & River Trust

Poem by Ian McMillan:
Poet, comedian & broadcaster, Vice President of the Poetry Society.

Marking the launch of the Canal & River Trust in 2012, the Poetry Society commissioned poet Ian McMillan to write a new poem in celebration of our canals. There's no shortage of inspiration when you live near a canal, McMillan explains: "I used to see the line of an old canal glinting in the sun near my house in Barnsley like the line of a poem, a slow poem that you took your time with, a poem that went through many drafts, lots of history's verses..."

WHERE
The poem is designed to be performed! There's a recording of Ian McMillan reading his poem on:

www.canalandrivertrust.org.uk   www.poetrysociety.org.uk

MORE INFO
More about Ian McMillan and his poetry. www.ian-mcmillan.co.uk

Visit our website for more about the 100 Treasures, and tell us your favourite treasure www.coolcanals.com/100treasures

CANAL LIFE

The canal tells you stories
The canal sings you songs
They hang in that space
Between memory and water

Once saw a narrowboat raised up,
Like it was cutting through the air,
Between two grass walls and the road below
Like it was sliding through history,
And a tiny vole swam across the water
So a tiny vole swam through history.

The canal tells you stories
The canal sings you songs

Once saw a man floating belly up in a canal
Like he was in the bath. He shouted
'This is the life' as I passed by on a narrowboat;
The sky was reflected in the surface
And we tied up in the places the map never showed us,
The man floating by, making ripples on the surface.

They hang in that space
Between memory and water

Once got waved at by a jogger as I stood gongoozling
On the towpath; her running gave rhythm
To the early afternoon, dog-strollers and kids
Who'd rather be here than sitting in school.
To gongoozle is to stand and watch narrowboats pass
And a canal is a lesson, a water-based school.

The canal tells you stories
The canal sings you songs

Once these canals were information highways
If coal and iron can be information,
And I think they can be. And there are bridges,
Pub gardens, the laughter of children
As they walk by the water; and the canals
Turn us all into curious children.

They hang in that space
Between memory and water

Once is never enough for a canal, I reckon;
You need to go back and see it again,
And sail it again, and smell it again, and
Touch it again; canals run through our veins
Like they stroll through this country
Like blood through our veins.

The canal tells you stories
The canal sings you songs
They hang in that space
Between memory and water

2 PONTCYSYLLTE AQUEDUCT
Showpiece of Britain's canals & a World Heritage Site

Eighteen pillars stretch to the heavens to suspend a great bathtub of water in the sky, making sane people swear that narrowboats can fly.

Pontcysyllte Aqueduct was built by William Jessop and Thomas Telford to carry the Llangollen Canal across the River Dee, and ever since the aqueduct opened in 1805, narrowboats without wings have flown over the river in a cast iron trough held up by stone pillars.

ABOVE: Boaters and walkers united in fear on the Aqueduct

Each of the pillars is still fixed by an unnerving concoction of lime and ox blood and the ironwork of the trough is sealed by a mad potion of Welsh flannel and lead dunked in boiling sugar. Luckily, not everyone who visits knows this and hysteria is kept at bay. But the boldest truth is exposed for all to see as 127ft of fresh air holds white-faced boaters and walkers above the valley of the River Dee.

Sheer drops menace the vertiginous and non-vertiginous alike and wide-eyed people are compelled to share jokes of fear with people they've never met before as they hip bump together on the snake thin path. Boats embark on a no going back vertical bungee ride in a boat in the sky. Their thrill is sheer drops that haven't been spoiled by railings and the cold comfort of a cloud teasing journey spanning 1007ft.

The Llangollen Canal was built before engines ruled the world, and over 200 years ago horses pulled boats across the canal in the sky. The railings at the entrance of the aqueduct have been left with grooves carved from the ropes of giant horses that once trod trustingly over a ridiculously brave manmade structure.

The story of the unpronounceable aqueduct is more than a history of who built it and why: it is the drama it has created, and continues to create, as anyone who crosses plays their part in the living documentary of a terrifying marvel.

Even for those too trapped by a rigor of fear to venture across, the Pontcysyllte Aqueduct is the ultimate must-see event of Britain's canals.

ABOVE: The trip boat, 'Thomas Telford', taking passengers for the ride of their lives across the Aqueduct

WHERE
Llangollen Canal
Trevor Basin, nr. Llangollen. OS SJ270421

MORE INFO
Boat Trips
'Eirlys', Jones the Boats
In Trevor Basin. 45-minute cruises across the aqueduct and back with full commentary. Seating is inside the narrowboats with clear window views (if you dare look). Luckily for the vertiginous, there's a well-stocked bar on board.
www.canaltrip.co.uk

'Thomas Telford'
Cruises the canal from Llangollen with the crossing of Pontcysyllte Aqueduct as its highlight.
www.horsedrawnboats.co.uk

Built by Thomas Telford and William Jessop, Pontcysyllte Aqueduct was completed in 1805. The Aqueduct and 11 miles of the Llangollen Canal stretching from Horseshoe Falls beyond Llangollen to Chirk Aqueduct were designated as a UNESCO World Heritage Site in 2009.

Pontcysyllte UNESCO World Heritage Site www.pontcysyllte-aqueduct.co.uk   whc.unesco.org/en/list

Local legend has it that one local, unmarried, young man lost his life building the aqueduct. It is believed he was called George Davies but it is hoped that one day his name will be known for sure so that a fitting memorial can be put in place.

Visit our website for more about the 100 Treasures, and tell us your favourite treasure www.coolcanals.com/100treasures

3 HEDGEROW
Nature lines a manmade route

Place boundaries can be blunt marks of paint on the ground, faint dots on the map or a telling signpost on the landscape. They define any place as different from the next. But along the canals of Britain, more than 600 miles of hedgerows create a historic boundary of sensory significance. The canal hedgerow is the border between the outside world and the waterways world.

Almost every way you turn in Britain, there's a chance to spy a long line of foliage concealing the secrets of the canal from outside eyes. For leisure- seeking canal folk, it's a barrier from noise and motion, a shield to escape the reality of fast living. However, history reveals that hedges were often planted by the original canal builders to protect the two worlds from each other for more mercenary reasons. Canals were the trade routes of the Industrial Revolution and arrived controversially, much as a new motorway would today. Every attempt had to be made to hide the uncouth 'water-scar' on the landscape from the genteel eyes of landowners. Canals never intended to be the havens for happiness they now strive to be, and towpaths were the mere domain of working boat horses. Hard-skinned boat families accompanied the filthy freight traffic and were labelled outcasts by 'decent' society. Such social snobbery of the original canal era probably helped leave a legacy of secrecy, and nurtured a hidden culture that has evolved magnificently into today's quiet waterways community. Remarkably, it's still the hedgerow that shelters the soul of the linear waterway from whatever noise blights from beyond.

The modern hedgerow brings the countryside into the city. And as sprawling urbanism gobbles green belts at will, canals with their green hedges are becoming vital linear parks for the wellbeing of local people - joggers, walkers, cyclists, boaters, picnickers and toddlers feeding the ducks.

Canals treat the visitor to the unquantifiable joys of nature - hawthorn, rosehip, elder, blackberry, hazel - the fruits of our nation line the canals; and, as the seasons turn, each has its time to stand out.

May dances with exuberance as hawthorn blossom brings the widest white smile of spring. In Celtic tree lore, hawthorn was said to be the symbol of fertility, and its wedding garlands put on a show along the canals, as if to fanfare the start of another holiday boating season. When the fuss of spring calms down, summer melts into elder flowers and red berries, before robust autumn huddles up with its hazel nuts cosily preparing for winter. The hedgerow wraps the canal up in a calendar of comforts. And, as if nature had told them to, narrowboats find places to tie up their ropes and snuggle together before the worst weather arrives.

Canal hedgerows are home to countless creatures from bats to beetles, providing platters of food and a comfy shelter for birds, mice, rabbits, invertebrates, reptiles, amphibians - all important for biodiversity. But hedgerows can't be taken for granted. During the early years of mechanical progress, most of rural England lost its precious hedgerows as they were ripped out to make way for bigger fields, bigger machinery, bigger gains. Luckily, the canals protected their hedgerows, and with passionate conservation in modern years, nature has been allowed to keep its living heritage.

Swaying with thorns to protect and blossom to uplift, the hedgerow's job stands still in time. It's a living presence, a protector, a divider and a giver of berries, blossom and leaves - a continually changing ecosystem. And while water, boats and eye-popping engineering marvels buff the 'USP' of our inland waterways, the humble hedgerow remains the canal's bountiful companion.

ABOVE: Lush May hawthorn blossom lining the Worcester & Birmingham Canal near Hanbury

WHERE
On canals throughout Britain
The canals are open all day every day - just find your local canal. Go in spring for the exuberant white of the hawthorn blossom or in autumn for the red berries.

MORE INFO
To estimate the age of a hedgerow: track a 30-yard stretch of hedgerow and count the different shrubs and tree species (not including bramble or climbers). Multiply that number by 100 and that gives an approximate age for the hedgerow.

Visit our website for more about the 100 Treasures, and tell us your favourite treasure www.coolcanals.com/100treasures

4 NEPTUNE'S STAIRCASE
A journey of gods

The Roman god of the sea bellows over the Caledonian Canal from Neptune's Staircase - Scotland's spectacular staircase flight of 8 locks. Neptune's Staircase was built to allow ocean-going vessels to take giant steps, up a rise of 64ft, from the west side of Scotland, and to be carried inland by canal, leaving the sea behind. Neptune's Staircase presents itself with sensory overload - it's not just the longest staircase flight in Britain, it's a flamboyant feat of engineering swept into a panoramic melodrama by Highland mists and the moods of Ben Nevis peering straight down over the flight.

Telford was a Scotsman and the Caledonian Canal was his Highland baby. Its route slices coast to coast from Corpach near Fort William in the west to Inverness in the east, on a journey of sublime pleasures. The origins of the route began around 400 million years ago, when two land masses crashed together to form the Great Glen. In his century, Telford's plan linked the lochs of the Great Glen to create a coast to coast canal - and Neptune's Staircase was his masterpiece of engineering to bridge water levels from sea to canal.

This manmade route is wild to the core, with a terrain that holds echoes of clan pipes, Napoleonic Wars and nature. Before the canal arrived, sailing ships had to endure the seas around the vicious north coast to travel from one side of Scotland to the other. It was during the wretched era of Highland Clearances that work on the canal began, and the construction created bitter-sweet employment during those troubled times. The canal was originally intended to provide a safe short cut for the navy during the Napoleonic Wars, but the build was only completed in 1822 after Napoleon had already been defeated. The canal was criticised for its slow build and errors. Telford's plans had allowed for 20ft depth, and yet the canal only scraped a mere 14ft when it opened, making it too shallow for many of the new larger sailing ships. The canal had to be closed between 1843 and 1847 for major reconstruction.

The canal today is a celebration of success. Neptune's Staircase takes around 1½ hours to work through by boat, and much longer to linger over as a sightseer. Originally, it was hand powered, taking 126 complete turns of the capstans for every boat that passed through. Now the lock gates (each weighing 22 tons) are operated by a hydraulic system, and the remains of the capstan mechanism can be leisurely admired in remembrance of the formidable task for those canal ancestors.

Neptune's Staircase is a monument for past times and an active servant of today's tourism. It makes no pretence of modesty, with monster waterfalls that cascade to and from its mighty lock chambers. Big boats dwarf any brave small boats that dare join them on their passage. This is living heritage at its best and the staircase still showcases the canal's crowning glory - the sight of ships scrambling into Scotland's Highlands.

WHERE
Caledonian Canal
Corpach. OS NN098766
Walk up the flight and if you're lucky, watch how the lockkeeper helps boats through the flight overlooked by Ben Nevis.

MORE INFO
Neptune's Staircase is a Scheduled Monument.

Fort William & Corpach Tourist Info www.visit-fortwilliam.co.uk

Visit Scottish Canals for more info about the canal. www.scottishcanals.co.uk

---

Visit our website for more about the 100 Treasures, and tell us your favourite treasure www.coolcanals.com/100treasures

RIGHT: The lockkeeper helping a boat through the Staircase

5 BRINDLEY'S GRAND CROSS
An ambitious plan

The success of Britain's first canal, built for the Duke of Bridgewater's mines, created a rush of interest as other businessmen wanted Brindley to build individual canals for them. Brindley had the foresight to know that a lot of local canals would not be as purposeful as one well-planned national network. His Grand Cross was a plan to build canals to connect the main four rivers - the River Thames, Severn, Trent and Mersey. This brave plan meant London would be connected to the rapidly growing industries of northern England and the crazy era of Canal Mania was born.

James Brindley grew up on a farm in the north of England and started his career as an apprentice to a millwright. Brindley married in 1765, and had 2 daughters, and his reputation began to grow. He had worked on a silk mill and several other projects that built his reputation for good work, and his crowning success was building the Bridgewater Canal. The country hurled itself at his feet and everyone seemed to want a canal built by Brindley. He was destined to a lifetime of overwork.

His plan for the Grand Cross was a revolution in the transport system of Britain. Four canals: the Trent & Mersey Canal from the River Trent at Shardlow to the Bridgewater Canal at Preston Brook; the Staffordshire & Worcestershire Canal from the River Severn at Stourport to the Trent & Mersey Canal at Great Haywood; the Oxford Canal from Oxford on the River Thames to Hawkesbury Junction where it met the Coventry Canal which linked to the Trent & Mersey Canal at Fradley.

The nation's new transport route was cause for unbridled excitement for the greatest entrepreneurs of the era. In Stoke-on-Trent Josiah Wedgwood could abandon the use of slow and clumsy packhorses and carry his fragile pots by boat instead. In his pleasure, in 1766, Wedgwood cut the first sod of earth for the canal and Brindley reputedly carried it away in a barrow!

Brindley's canals were narrow with locks set to the maximum size of 70ft by 7ft. The Harecastle Tunnel (2,880yds/2658m) was an expensive section to build and it probably influenced Brindley's decision to keep his canals narrow. His early canals weren't adventurous with lots of aqueducts and exuberant built marvels like later canals were - instead they were winding, and mostly flat, as they followed the natural contours of the land.

The Grand Cross plan was a resounding success and the major trunk became the first water road 'motorway' system. Brindley was in such constant demand his health suffered. When something difficult troubled him at work, he went to bed to think in peace. Writing and drawing weren't his chosen way of working since he was scarcely literate. His notes were often painful phonetic scribbles with no reverence to his genius. His pioneering labours were without the help of Ordnance Survey maps (the first OS map was 1801) and the task was never easy.

In the last eight years of his life he struggled with diabetes, and ill heath finally hurled a fatal blow when he was out in bad weather surveying a branch canal from Etruria to Froghall In 1772. After sleeping in a damp bed in a local inn, his condition deteriorated and he died aged 55 at home. It is said he died of overwork. He was laid to rest in Newchapel in Staffordshire where his memorial inscription describes him as 'canal engineer', but his reputation gave him the majestic title the 'Father of English Canals'.

RIGHT: James Brindley
'Engineer to his Grace the Duke of Bridgewater'
(National Waterways Archive)

WHERE

On canals throughout Britain

The canals are open all day every day. James Brindley was involved in the planning and construction of almost 400 miles of Britain's canals, including the Bridgewater Canal, the Trent & Mersey Canal and the Staffordshire & Worcestershire Canal, yet few were completed during his lifetime.

Artefacts relating to James Brindley are kept in the National Waterways Archive in the National Waterways Museum at Ellesmere Port. Access to the Archive is FREE but must be prebooked. T:0151 3555017 www.nwm.org.uk

MORE INFO

Brindley preferred to follow the contours of the land rather than the most direct route, avoiding the cuttings and tunnels used by engineers such as Thomas Telford. One of his greatest ideas was the use of clay puddling for the base and sides of the canals to keep them watertight, a system still used today.

There are contrasting statues of Brindley - a formal monument to him at Etruria, by the junction of the Trent & Mersey and Caldon Canals, shows an upright man with his theodolite (an instrument which he used for surveying canals), another in Coventry Canal basin captures Brindley in action, toiling over papers on his desk.

Visit our website for more about the 100 Treasures, and tell us your favourite treasure www.coolcanals.com/100treasures

6 ROPE
The rugged art & skill of every boater

Ropes are the rugged adventure, the raw romance, and the practical panache of the canals in action. Boaters learn the skills of using ropes, yet the rewards are more than function: there's something seductively rustic about ropes that fills the senses with wet, hempy smells and tactile dreams of wild outdoor derring-do.

Ropes have been used since prehistoric times and the earliest ropes were probably twists of plants that had been braided together. China made rope out of hemp as far back as 2800BC, and impressions of rope have been found in fired clay in Europe estimated to be from 28,000 years ago - but it was the Ancient Egyptians who were the first to document tools for ropemaking.

Rope has been the servant of power throughout time and travel. The battles of empires, which were won on the high seas, owe their victory to the ropes that made their vessels sail; and during the era of the first canal trade routes, before engines had been invented, a horse could not have towed his boat without rope.

Most ropes were once made from natural fibres such as hemp, sisal, manila, but manmade fibre stole a giant portion of the market with the development of nylon that was water resistant and defiant of rot.

Boaters learn and use special knots to secure their boats to mooring dollies and rings all across the networks, and in doing so, they unceremoniously become keepers of the living heritage of Britain's canals. Knots have held vessels to canal banks since the birth of the canals, and when a holidaymaker learns to tie his first mooring knot, beyond the unquantifiable fun, he is re-enacting history from the great days of the first Canal Mania.

As with most great systems, it is often the smallest elements that get taken for granted. An unassuming few feet of rope is a must for canal boating. Towing ropes, mooring knots, fenders and more. Every size and shape of canal boat owes everything to the ropes that pull, protect and secure it.

Mighty millions of pounds are scraped into the annual pot needed to help keep canals open for navigation, and to protect the vital role boats play in the real life of the waterways. Every boater and towpath tourist cheers, "canals were made for boats". True - yet, without ropes, boats would be left in hopeless chaos. Ropes are essential in order to maintain the simple process of water travel.

WHERE
On canals throughout Britain
The canals are open all day every day - just find your local canal.

MORE INFO
Boat fenders on narrowboats are traditionally made of rope. Learn how to tie knots or make fenders - full listings of craftsmen and women creating ropework and rope fenders on Britain's canals can be found in our online directory.

www.coolcanals.com

Visit our website for more about the 100 Treasures, and tell us your favourite treasure www.coolcanals.com/100treasures

ABOVE: Moored up on the Gloucester & Sharpness Canal
RIGHT: A tangle of ropes

7 MUSEUM OF LONDON DOCKLANDS
How Britain traded with the world

Canary Wharf dazzles the London Skyline with Cesar Pelli's tower, better known as One Canada Square, which was once confidently the tallest building in Britain until the Shard muscled in. One Canada Square has its own attraction but, only a short walk away, the cooing of designer shopping is replaced by the intense drama of London's Dockland heritage. Here, the important history of every era of the city is housed in the Dockland's Museum that sits quietly on the waterside. The tranquil exterior of this museum is a decoy to the giddy experience housed inside.

The River Thames and the oceans beyond have always raged with an island's defence strategies, but as much as the water is an invader's route, it is also the trade route that once helped build the British Empire. By the late 1700s the River Thames was overcrowded with merchants' ships arriving from around the world. As they moored on the river to allow small boats (called 'lighters') to ferry their cargoes to the shore, the Thames became jammed with chaos; tall masts waved over the water and boats butted starboard to portside. Rogues didn't miss the opportunity of feeding the lucrative black market business from the precarious system of goods being loaded and unloaded from ship to shore. West India Merchants were so furious about their losses that they demanded a secure dock was built. The engineers William Jessop, John Rennie and Ralph Walker took up the baton, and London Docklands became the largest structure of its kind in the world at that time.

A world trade route was opened up by the relationship between the canals and the Docklands. Cargoes from ships were transferred into canal boats to be distributed along the Regent's Canal and the Grand Union Canal at Paddington to be carried further inland to the Midlands.

Coal, timber, cocoa, exotic fruits, tea and other cargo arrived in the Docklands, and warehouses along the quayside stored goods safely away from those opportunist scoundrels of the black market. Only two of the original warehouses have survived and the museum is housed in one of them. Exhibitions over several floors tell London's story eloquently, without sparing any emotion between the lightest joy to the darkest shame. London was the fourth biggest slave trading port in the world after Rio de Janeiro, Bahia and Liverpool. The vile truth of ships arriving with 'cargoes' of slaves is told in images and words that are uncomfortable to ingest, and even more uncomfortable to ignore. The round table at which William Wilberforce and others sat to discuss the abolition of slavery is a touching exhibit and a showpiece of hope.

Each floor of the museum takes the visitor back to a different time. One of the highlights is a fascinating model of the first London Bridge depicted from around 1440. Another fascinating feature is the dark alleyways of a life-like 'Sailortown' where multisensory effects immerse the visitor in a cobblestoned grotto with drunken sailors, pirates and merry rum-slinging characters.

From Roman settlers to Britain's latest prime minister, the museum tells a local story embedded with global connections. Fires, strikes, hangings and murders, overcrowding, the politics of power and war fill a museum that is classy, informative, entertaining and free!

In the 1960s, when it was no longer needed for its original purpose, Docklands closed and the area seemed destined to fester like an East End Untouchable, but when the area was rejuvenated, a deliberate twist of fate transformed the Museum in London Docklands into a must-see attraction.

ABOVE: Museum of London Docklands is housed in historic Warehouse No.1

WHERE

North Quay, West India Quay
London. OS TQ372805
Open daily. FREE admission. Gift shop. As well as its permanent galleries, the museum runs a schedule of events, exhibitions and occasional courses. Venue hire. Wheelchair access.

MORE INFO

The museum is housed in Warehouse No. 1, one of only two survivors of the original nine Georgian warehouses erected on the North Quay of West India Quay by the West India Dock Company to store sugar, rum and coffee – the produce of slave plantations in the Caribbean. The other warehouses were destroyed during World War II in September 1940. Warehouse No.1 is Grade I-listed and was originally built as a 'low' warehouse in 1802-1804 but had an extra two storeys added in 1827 by John Rennie.

T:020 7001 9844 www.museumoflondon.org.uk/Docklands

Visit our website for more about the 100 Treasures, and tell us your favourite treasure www.coolcanals.com/100treasures

8 FRIENDSHIP
The last No 1

Boats would just be boats without the people who crew them. Friendship is the aptly named boat that was once both a home and a way of earning a living for two much-loved characters of the cut, Joe and Rose Skinner.

Working narrowboats were mostly owned by companies such as Fellows Morton & Clayton or the Grand Union Canal Carrying Company (GUCC), but there were some boats that were owned by the families that crewed them. They were known as the No 1s, and much pride was associated with these boats.

Friendship was a No 1 owned by Joe and Rose Skinner. It was one of the last boats to be built by Sephtons of Hawkesbury Junction, and the Skinners bought her in 1924 for £300 (with a deposit of £140 and instalments thereafter of 10 shillings a week). Friendship was a 70ft unpowered boat, and the Skinners earned a living carrying commercial cargo along the canal with their boat that was pulled by a mule. In 1928 they bought a second boat called Elizabeth (Mrs S's middle name). The two boats were towed in tandem by a pair of mules called Dolly and Dick. Elizabeth was sold in 1937, but the Skinners continued to work, mostly trundling up and down the Coventry and Oxford Canals carrying coal from coal fields in the East Midlands to businesses in Banbury.

During the busy era of Canal Mania, donkeys, mules and horses were all vital members of a team as they towed working boats across the landscape and through endless lock flights. The dependency was so fundamental to the lifestyle that a boat family often saw their horse as a member of the family. Joe is said to have loved all animals and when Dolly, his last mule, died, he retired.

Joe and Rose Skinner were destined to be written down in history as the last No 1 boaters, and even before they had retired the couple enjoyed mini-fame as they were frequently interviewed by press keen to tell the novel story of these two fabulous canal characters. It was reported by one paper that, from the 1960s, when the Skinners eventually had a house to live in, they still trotted off down the towpath at bedtime to snuggle up to sleep in the tiny boatman's cabin aboard Friendship. Joe is quoted as saying in a newspaper article, "Lor, bless you, we couldn't sleep between four walls. We've got to hear the water slapping against the sides and feel the gentler roll of the old boat before we can sleep a wink." The relationship between a No 1 boat and its owners doesn't wither with retirement.

The Skinners were much liked within the canal community, and Joe's weather-beaten face sparkled with cheer until he died in 1975, aged 82. Rose died a year later, aged 77. They are buried together under a cherry tree in the Windmill Cemetery at Longford.

Friendship lives on to keep her owners' story alive. The Coventry Canal Society bought the boat in 1977 with an appeal to raise funds to buy her on behalf of the Boat Museum (now the National Waterways Museum). At her new home in the museum, she was kept afloat despite the horrors of her leaky condition. But eventually, in 1981, it was decided that Friendship had to be housed inside the museum to protect her from festering mud worm and the threat of sinking.

How did the museum managed to haul a rotting vessel from the water and carry it up to the first floor to the exhibition area? The saga is now a legendary tale to be passed on as another zany achievement in the life story of Friendship. The boat was cut into two sections for the manoeuvre. A mad idea that was supremely successful. Friendship now sits as the centre piece inside the museum, enjoying her retirement in safe care.

ABOVE: Historic photograph of Joe & Rose Skinner onboard Friendship (National Waterways Archive)

The boatman's cabin has been carefully protected to retain paintwork from the 1950s that was done at the famous Tooley's Boatyard, and Tony Lewery (a much respected maestro of canal-boat painting today) repainted the cabin exterior to restore it to its former glory.

The museum invites visitors to climb inside Friendship and peer with respect, and awe, into the tiny boatman's cabin that holds the most dear secrets of Joe and Rose. The intimacy is moving, and a recording of Mrs Skinner chatting about her life adds to the privilege of the moment. The only thing missing is the piping hot cup of tea Mrs S would have surely brewed for her visitors.

WHERE
Shropshire Union Canal
Ellesmere Port. OS SJ405771
Friendship is on display in the National Waterways Museum in Ellesmere Port. Open daily. Café and gift shop. Admission charge. Wheelchair access to most areas.

T:0151 3555017 www.nwm.org.uk

MORE INFO
Friendship is listed on the National Register of Historic Vessels (NRHV).

www.nationalhistoricships.org.uk

Visit our website for more about the 100 Treasures, and tell us your favourite treasure www.coolcanals.com/100treasures

9 JACK O' THE LOCKS
The people's sculpture

My favourite treasures - chosen by John Bridgeman CBE TD DL:
Vice Chairman of British Waterways and Trustee of the Canal & River Trust.
"Jack O' The Locks at Sowerby is a wonderful 'Heritage Sculpture'. It exemplifies
so much about our canals - a local man, out in all weathers, the admiring boy
doing what he can, both joined in the noble art of hard manual work."

At its best, Public Art along Britain's canals reaches intimately into history and plucks out the spirit of living heritage - a visual tool for conserving the culture of the past and, at the same time, enhancing today's canal environment. Jack O' The Locks is an iconic sculpture, greeting visitors at the entrance to Sowerby Bridge Wharf.

Two bronze figures are caught in a moment, working the black and white arm of an old lock gate. The arch of a little bronze boy's back is taut, propelling innocent-energy to his eager bronze hands that push the lock

ABOVE: Sowerby Bridge Wharf is home to the hireboat company Shire Cruisers and a host of bars and cafés

arm with tender might. Sharing the task, a weather-worn patriarch looks over him with warmth. As a work of art, the two figures occupy the eye, yet it's the space that separates them that tugs on the heart of the voyeur. That void is packed to the brim with the eternal union of generations, taking any audience on a rollercoaster ride, peeling emotions from the basics of love and nurture, to nostalgia, pride and hope. Even a surprising dose of patriotism slips in through the backdoor of your mind as the figures ask you to respect their hard day's graft that once led an Empire.

Jack O' The Locks explicitly portrays the story of the old lockkeeper of Sowerby Bridge but, as any great sculpture that is set in a public space should, it implicitly commands concentric stories of the environment within which it sits.

Sowerby Bridge Wharf was once an important place where two canals met. The Rochdale Canal is a robust Pennine rambler that was originally constructed for vessels up to 72ft long. It met the Calder & Hebble Navigation at Sowerby Bridge, where cargo had to be transhipped to shorter boats. Bulk loads of salt, cotton, wool, coal, timber, limestone and general wares were stored in warehouses here. The historic warehouses that tower behind Jack, speak as ambassadors for the struggle for survival that canals have had to overcome since the railways first arrived. Sowerby Bridge Wharf and its 18th-century canal buildings were once left crumbling from neglect until HRH Prince Charles and the Prince's Regeneration Trust stepped in to help. A decade of work (in partnership with English Heritage, Yorkshire Forward, British Waterways - now the Canal & River Trust - and others) helped restore the wharf which has become a hive of leisure facilities, workshops and a canal boat wet-dock. Sowerby Bridge is busy again with the hubbub of tourists who turn up each year to go boating, shopping, wining and dining or simply sightseeing with an ice-cream. Regeneration did its bit, and this charismatic pocket of Yorkshire says the canals are loved again.

Success over adversity and the power of belief is the enduring message that clings in the cobblestones and corners of this place - and Jack O' The Locks, in solid silence, passes on the root sentiment that keeps past generations and new generations connected.

ABOVE: The sculpture guards the entrance to Sowerby Bridge Wharf

WHERE
Rochdale Canal / Calder & Hebble Navigation
Sowerby Bridge. OS SE064237
It's there permanently in the open air so visit when you like!

MORE INFO
Roger Burnett once worked in engineering design, before launching a fulltime career as an artist. He originally worked from a studio on a canal boat and went to the canals of France to make a living, then later moved to the Caribbean.

An amazing mix of businesses and individuals collectively raised funds for the commissioned work by artist Roger Burnett. A 'roll of honour' plaque listing these people and friends is mounted on the sculpture. As such, the fundraisers have become part of the sculpture they asked to be created.

Visit our website for more about the 100 Treasures, and tell us your favourite treasure www.coolcanals.com/100treasures

10 CANAL BRIDGE
Beauty in purpose

When canals were first built they sliced fields in half and cut through private property; so the canal bridge was a vital link route over the water. Now, the bridge has become more than just a structure that is used to get past an obstacle, it has become an object of beauty itself.

The tranquillity of canals is defined by seductively shaped arches that wrap over the water. Every region is unique with the different colours of local stone creating its own look. There's pale Welsh stone, Bath stone, red sandstone and dark Pennine rock, and any shade between. And delicious London brick does its own thing too.

ABOVE: 'Snake' bridge on the Macclesfield Canal

There are lift-up bridges, opening bridges and, most commonly, the single arch bridge. The canal usually squeezes into a narrower route with a tight towpath clinging to the water. The narrowing is called the bridge 'ole and has often been the curse of tillersmen past and present.

Working horses that originally pulled narrowboats had to use bridges to cross to the other side of the canal when the towpath did. The ropes had to be unhitched for the boat to pass under the bridge while the horse crossed over it. The process was time consuming, costing businesses money, so some canal companies designed bridges with clever ways to resolve the problem. 'Split bridges' (such as on the Stratford Canal) have rope-sized slits straight through the arch of the bridge, and 'roving bridges' (such as at Great Haywood Junction) swirled to the towpath to keep the ropes centred to the boat with no need to unhitch. A distinctive feature on the Macclesfield Canal is the 'snake bridge' which twists from the arch onto the towpath like a dramatic sculpture. Across the networks there are also swing bridges (Llangollen Canal), concrete bridges, the famous cast-iron Horseley bridges (such as Hawkesbury Junction), and Rennie's ornate bridges (Kennet & Avon Canal).

History hides under bridges in the gouge marks from the horses' strain of towing ropes, and lie alongside modern scrapes of narrowboat paint. The bridge is part of the life of the waterways, it is the punctuation of the water, and a symbol of the idyllic landscape - and probably not coincidentally, the feature that the swan guards in the new Canal & River Trust logo.

LOCATION
On canals throughout Britain
The canals are open all day every day - just find your local canal.

MORE INFO
The smooth cobbles on the ramps of canal bridges were usually studded with elevated bricks to help stop the working horses from slipping (and are quite helpful for walkers and boaters today!)

Visit our website for more about the 100 Treasures, and tell us your favourite treasure www.coolcanals.com/100treasures

RIGHT: The Grade II-listed Linacre Bridge on the restored Droitwich Canals was built by James Brindley c.1771

11 PURTON HULKS
A whispering graveyard of boats

The Gloucester & Sharpness Canal sidles alongside the Severn estuary, with its tame waters following the moody route of a river. The River Severn has the second highest tidal range in the world, which was the reason the more navigable manmade canal was built in the first place; yet in an ironic twist, over the years the river slowly channelled too close, threatening the canal's survival. A fateful high tide in 1909 coincided with a savage storm, and wild waves reared to breach the banks, draining the water from the canal. Drastic action was needed, and an unexpected solution gave the canals something that has become one of its most dramatic wonders - Purton Hulks.

An immediate plea went out for help and, in a bid to secure the banks of the canal, retired boats and old wrecks were towed up the estuary and beached on the muddy shores of the river. For over half a century, more boats were piled on top of each other in the hopes of slowing down further erosion. Wooden sailing craft, steel barges and any old unwanted boats were all dumped onto the banks near Purton, until a barrier formed with thick silt settling in and around the hulks. It's now officially recognised as the largest cluster of historic maritime boats in Britain. Most of the 81 boats counted in the graveyard have been lost under silt and decayed, but 30 can still be seen.

ABOVE: 'Dursley' - built in 1926, beached in 1963

Whole bodies and bits and bobs of craft are scattered around the graveyard; and sometimes there are just plaques of remembrance. Amongst the most striking are the monster concrete barges from World War II that snuggle with dead weight into their resting place. These concrete vessels were built when steel was in short supply during the war, and as they slumber on the silty banks of the estuary, it's almost inconceivable that they ever floated.

Another boat with a wild story is the Katherine Ellen, a 127ft schooner. She was a gun-runner for the IRA until the Royal Navy impounded her in 1921. All that's left of her now is her bilge pump.

The trows were once the main sailing ships that carried commerce along the river, and many of the wrecks hold the stories and ghosts of those hardy vessels. Edith was a trow built in 1901, and her 75ft by 17ft remains were laid to rest in the boat graveyard around 1963. Edith endured a lifetime of storms and struggles and eventually sank after a collision, before being retired to Purton. Edith's tale rambles into eternity with superstitious overture: it's reputed that her engine was saved and stored, and many years later was fitted into a narrowboat that also sank (spooky).

Those who hunt through the Purton Hulks tread a whispering graveyard, where wrecks have wallowed like heroes with a purpose. The landscape has grown in and out of the bones of boats and tufts of grass sway from the carcasses of giants that saved the canal. Wet smells of old craft brush in the breeze, like lost soldiers in a battlefield; a rotting glory, this place is a tear jerker, dragging deep emotion from even the most armoured soul. Purton Hulks steal the heart of anyone who visits, with an uninhibited and extreme sentiment that rips the air - mournful, moving and painfully exciting.

ABOVE: The wreck of 'Rockby' - built in the 1890s, beached in 1946, with a background of the River Severn

WHERE
Gloucester & Sharpness Canal
Purton. OS SO687044
The Purton Hulks are between the river Severn and the Gloucester & Sharpness Canal. There are no barriers or admission charges - simply visit and respect this special place.

MORE INFO
Part of the site has been awarded the status of SSSI (Site of Special Scientific Interest) and several of the boats are listed on the National Register of Historic Vessels (NRHV).

www.nationalhistoricships.org.uk

Friends of Purton www.friendsofpurton.org.uk

Visit our website for more about the 100 Treasures, and tell us your favourite treasure www.coolcanals.com/100treasures

My favourite treasure - chosen and written by Paul Atterbury:
Art historian, writer, transport enthusiast and expert on BBC Television's
Antiques Roadshow, Vice President of the Waterways Trust (now merged with
British Waterways into Canal & River Trust)

In 1969 the British Waterways Board commissioned a new series of guides from a small London company, Robert Nicholson Publications. These, the first fully comprehensive guides to the canals and waterways of England and Wales, reflected a new attitude at BWB that welcomed and encouraged the development of the waterway leisure market.

A colleague, Andrew Darwin, and I were given the task of carrying out the research and fieldwork for the guides, which I was also to write and edit. Over the next three years we explored every inch of every canal and waterway under BWB's control, including ones that were then derelict, such as the Kennet & Avon and the Montgomery, by boat, on foot, by bicycle, by motorcycle and by car. We recorded details of the landscape, towns and villages, pubs, boatyards and other features of interest along the route. This formed the basis of the text that accompanied the maps and everything was assembled by Nicholson's cartographer on specially drawn maps that depicted the waterways and their environment in geographical rather than linear form.

It was an immense and generally enjoyable task, undertaken in the pre-computer, pre-digital, pre-mobile phone age. Andrew and I sometimes communicated by telegram. The working tools were Ordnance Survey maps, paper, pens, pencils and a typewriter, and the research sources were the British Waterways Board and various specialist guides, such as Pevsner's Buildings of England series.

There were four guides in the series, covering the South East, the North West, the South West and the North East. Later, a fifth one, covering the Midland area in greater detail, was added to the series, which was complete by 1974. The work gave me a taste for canals and I had a number of canal holidays on hire boats through the 1970s. In 1981 I bought my own boat, Ibis, which kept us busy for the next fifteen years. Throughout this time I had ample opportunity to use the Nicholson guides.

ABOVE: The first four Nicholson's Guides to the Waterways

Nicholson's Guides to the Waterways are still available today, having been regularly updated, and are still the standard guides for canal and waterway users. The modern ones are clearly the direct descendants of the ones we produced and when I dip into them occasionally, and sometimes read my own words, all the adventures of forty years ago come flooding back. **PAUL ATTERBURY**

ABOVE: Paul Atterbury out researching for the Nicholson's Guides in the 1970s
ABOVE LEFT: Excerpt from the first Nicholson's Guide to the South East

WHERE

Almost every boat cruising the waterways has a well-used copy of a Nicholson Waterways Guide at hand near the tiller

Historic copies of the first Nicholson Guides are kept in the National Waterways Museum in Ellesmere Port.

www.nwm.org.uk

MORE INFO

Nicholson Waterways Guides are published by Collins, an imprint of HarperCollins. There are currently 8 in the series with the recent addition of the Norfolk Broads, and two are now also available in ebook format for Kindle.

www.harpercollins.co.uk

Visit our website for more about the 100 Treasures, and tell us your favourite treasure www.coolcanals.com/100treasures

13 ARKWRIGHT'S MILL
The first 'factory'

A tingle asks to be treasured as you stand on the spot where the Industrial Revolution was conceived. Cromford Mill, built by Richard Arkwright in 1771, was the world's first water-powered cotton spinning mill. A mill of monumental importance in the story of the world.

Britain's economic and social history is stamped on Arkwright-hallowed ground. Arkwright (1732-1792) was born in Preston, the son of a humble tailor. He died a rich man, knighted by King George III, and immortalised by his title as the 'father of the factory system'.

ABOVE: The Cromford Canal starts just a few yards from Arkwright's Mill. A walk along the towpath leads deeper into the Peak District

Arkwright invented the cotton spinning frame and launched the textile manufacturing industry on a new scale. His mill innovatively used machinery in 'one' building, with only the need of a relatively small and unskilled workforce, maximising production and profit. The factory was born, and his innovative template launched a revolution. The young mill escaped the rabid furore of the Luddites who, in fear of change, rampaged against 'the machine', sabotaging Britain's new factories with violence.

Despite years of success, fate took its turn and progress eventually caught up with the mill, forcing it to close. After serious shortages of water in 1840, the old mill buildings changed use into a brewery, a laundry, a cheese warehouse and other trades.

In 1922 the site was used as a works for paints and dyes. Finally, in 1979, the colour works closed down and the buildings were abandoned. The site was almost lost, until its full importance was uncovered as it was being cleared for demolition. It was awarded Grade I-listed status and became part of the Derwent Valley Mills World Heritage Site.

The Arkwright Society bought the mill in 1979 and rescued it so that the world could treasure its industrial heritage. Today the society is a formidable charity manned with volunteers who can be spotted in the guise of shop attendants, tour guides, administrative folk and welcoming smiles to anyone who turns up for a grand day out at Arkwright's Mill.

The main mill is currently under restoration, with plans for the ground floor to lead visitors through part of the 15-mile World Heritage Site from Matlock Bath to Derby. Some of the restored buildings conceal craft shops and the expected fodder for day trippers - shopping, eating, exhibitions and events mixed with a heritage tour of industry and transport, and a cuppa to keep the whole family happy.

Oddly, it's not unbecoming that an idyllic corner of the Peak District, where walkers and wildlife spotters like to go, is also a place where the Industrial Revolution began. The entire site screams with history and Arkwright's Mill is a magnificent showpiece of the world's first textile factory.

ABOVE: Cromford Mill - clusters of mill buildings surround the central courtyard

WHERE
Cromford Canal
Cromford. OS SK298569
Open daily all year. FREE admission (small parking charge). Restaurant, café and gift shops. Tours of Cromford Mill can be arranged (charge).

MORE INFO
Cromford Mill was built in 1771 by Richard Arkwright. It is Grade I-listed and part of the Derwent Valley Mills UNESCO World Heritage Site.

Arkwright Society T:01629 823256 www.arkwrightsociety.org.uk

Derwent Valley Mills UNESCO World Heritage Site www.derwentvalleymills.org   whc.unesco.org/en/list

Visit our website for more about the 100 Treasures, and tell us your favourite treasure www.coolcanals.com/100treasures

14 BUDE SEA LOCK
Where a canal tumbles onto the beach

When an inland waterway crashes into the sea, an explosion of emotion is bound to spill over at the meeting point of two different waters. A golden beach in Cornwall is the place where wild seafaring sailors bellow their salty windswept stories at whispering narrow tales from secret inland Britain. Two worlds rub together with lobster pots on the canal bank, and lonely cries of seagulls echoing across still water.

Few sights anywhere along Britain's canals seem as incongruously purposeful as Bude sea lock. When the tide is out, the great lock arms stretch over the dry sands of Summerleaze Beach, but when the tide is right, the canal tumbles into the sea.

When the Bude Canal originally opened in 1823, it was used for trade, carrying sand, limestone, coal and farm manures. It was later abandoned, but the 2-mile stretch from Bude to Helebridge has been made navigable again. The sea lock is its crowning glory: it was restored in 2000 and, as well as being one of only two in the UK opening directly on to the sea, it is also a Scheduled Ancient Monument.

The lock is set in a huge breakwater that protects and enhances the wharf area. Merciless seas constantly batter the lock and try to defeat the canal. In 2008, a storm wrenched one of the gates off its hinges, but it was repaired and the lock still defiantly works. Repairs are par for the course, but when the battle of the seas is won by a canal, the rewards are magnificent: the triumph of man over nature, in the simplicity of a canal lock. A Cornish treat.

WHERE
Bude Canal
Bude. OS SS203064

MORE INFO
The Sea Lock towers over Summerleaze Beach and, depending on how you time it with the tides, you'll either see small vessels stranded in the sand leading up to the lock, or the sea surrounding the lock on three sides.

Bude Sea Lock is Grade II-listed and a Scheduled Ancient Monument.

Bude Tourist Info & Canal Interpretation Centre www.visitbude.info

Visit our website for more about the 100 Treasures, and tell us your favourite treasure www.coolcanals.com/100treasures

ABOVE LEFT: The walls of the breakwater tower over the beach
RIGHT: The canal opens out into Summerleaze Beach

BOUNDARY MARKER
Undercover history

My favourite treasures - chosen and written by Nigel Crowe:
Head of Heritage for the Canal & River Trust

" **Waterways heritage is sometimes very subtle and not always easy to spot. Boundary furniture, for example, can lurk in hedgerows or on embankments, or right at the water's edge. It is possible to stand right next to it without realising its significance.**

Here and there, this boundary heritage still quietly demonstrates where the old canal companies held sway. Companies often had their own purpose-made designs for fences, gates and stiles and these were often stamped with the company name or initials. One example of this is the collection of consistently designed field and towpath gates found along the southern stretches of the Oxford Canal. Another is the occasional surviving wooden gate found on the present-day Llangollen and Shropshire Union canals, with the letters SUC (Shropshire Union Canal) punched into its woodwork. The iron punches that were used are still kept at Ellesmere Yard, an Aladdin's Cave of historic canal equipment.

Other items of boundary furniture include pre-cast concrete fence-posts, with company initials countersunk into them near their tops. Even harder to spot are stamped bricks, like those stamped BCN, which marked out the watery empire of the Birmingham Canal Navigations.

Most of the surviving boundary furniture of the waterways dates from the late 19th or early 20th centuries, before the 1948 nationalisation of Britain's canals swept away the old companies and led inevitably to the removal of their many distinguishing signs and markers.

Connoisseurs of such things will spot odd marks left by other organisations too, like the inscribed granite stones that denote the shared boundary of the River Lee Navigation and the War Department, or the WD, as it used to be known. "

NIGEL CROWE

WHERE
On canals throughout Britain
The canals are open all day every day - just find your local canal.

MORE INFO
Examples of historic boundary markers can be seen at Ellesmere Yard on the Shropshire Union Canal, in the National Waterways Museum at Ellesmere Port, and in other waterways museums such as Gloucester, London and Stoke Bruerne.

www.nwm.org.uk www.gloucesterwaterwaysmuseum.org.uk www.stokebruernecanalmuseum.org.uk

Visit our website for more about the 100 Treasures, and tell us your favourite treasure www.coolcanals.com/100treasures

RIGHT: Old Shropshire Union Canal boundary marker on the Montgomery Canal at Frankton Locks

16

BLACKCOUNTRYMAN
One of the canals' many historic trip boats

Black Country people were once the backbone of the Industrial Revolution - foundry workers, miners, glass turners; and the narrowboat with the namesake 'Blackcountryman' is a living tribute to the heritage of local people.

The Blackcountryman was built in 1948 by Harris Brothers in Netherton for Stewarts & Lloyds of Halesowen. It's thought to be the last full length 70ft boat built of riveted plates in the Black Country. In its more recent transformation, the Blackcountryman was fitted with a Lister diesel engine, but was originally unpowered and would have been towed by a tug, a horse, or even the might of a man.

The boat was used for trade on the Birmingham Canal Navigations (BCN) until it changed career to become a maintenance craft for British Waterways (now the Canal & River Trust). Like many of the historic canal boats that have survived, the Blackcountryman's raison d'etre had to be fluid with the times. In 1986 she was spectacularly converted to a passenger-carrying vessel for the Stoke-on-Trent National Garden Festival with the Queen Mother as prime guest.

In 1991 she changed hands and was restored, and spruced up for new purpose in Stourbridge. The boat's original crews would probably have raised their eyebrows over the addition of some fancies such as soft cushioned seats, side windows, loos, wheelchair access, taped music and (for goodness sake) a bar.

In her latest guise, the Blackcountryman is a trip boat that carries passengers from the distinctive round-walled Bonded Warehouse to Stourton and Kinver. The journey can be enjoyed as a floating escape to the quiet backwaters of the Midlands, or seen as a voyage to discover local heritage or even a brazen excuse to experience this historic boat at intimate quarters.

Like many of the best canal treasures, this boat refuses to retire. When the much respected Mick Bourne, the boat's last operator, retired, Tom Downing and his father Andy took up the baton. Tom became the youngest Boat Master in the country at the age of 18, and he and his boat, the Blackcountryman, both became national record breakers with local pride.

WHERE
Stourbridge Canal
Stourbridge. OS SO899848

MORE INFO
Afternoon cruises on the Blackcountryman run along the Stourbridge Canal and the Staffordshire & Worcestershire Canal. They also run special themed evening cruises. Dates and timings vary.

Blackcountryman is listed on the National Register of Historic Vessels (NRHV).

www.nationalhistoricships.org.uk

T:01384 375912 www.canalboattripsstourbridge.co.uk

There are trip boats operating all around Britain's canal network. Full listings of all canal trip boats in Britain can be found in our online directory. www.coolcanals.com

Visit our website for more about the 100 Treasures, and tell us your favourite treasure www.coolcanals.com/100treasures

ABOVE: Blackcountryman at Stourbridge
RIGHT: (left) 'Countess of Evesham' at Stratford-upon-Avon, (right) 'King Arthur' in Gloucester Docks, (bottom) 'Dragonfly' on the Monmouthshire & Brecon Canal

17

MIKRON THEATRE
Travelling drama

Under the blue skies of Greece, Mikron is the word for small - but in Britain, it's the apt name adopted by a tiny theatre company that travels the nation's waterways by canal boat. Mike Lucas was the founding member of Mikron in 1963, when his bold mission was to take theatre to unconventional venues and reach new, non-stereotypical, audiences. He set off in 1977 with a close team of actors and singers, in a narrowboat - and over 40 years later the success of Mikron has become an essential ingredient in Britain's waterways living heritage.

When Mikron first toured in the 1970s, Britain's canals were evolving through bitter-sweet times of neglect and new interest, as a redundant trade route struggled to become a leisure destination. Many canals were frighteningly rubbish-ridden and stinking in parts, yet Mike Lucas and his theatre company cruised wherever they might find an audience to entertain. Mike Lucas handed over the baton of running the theatre in 2005, and over the years the cast has kept vibrant and changing, while the ethos behind Mikron remains the same.

ABOVE: Mikron's cast for 2010's 'Striking the balance' aboard their narrowboat Tyseley before performing in Worcester Diglis Basin

When a theatre company turns up at a venue in a narrowboat, puts on a show and then leaves with as little fuss as they arrived, the impact can be shiveringly powerful. Mikron entertains with simplicity, captivating audiences who unwittingly freefall into a show that never needs the clutter of fancy props or luvvie-tiaras.

Mikron still performs at canalside pubs, festivals, village halls or even inside a canal tunnel if they are asked to. The zest of the cast shines brilliantly through stories that are effortlessly sharp, and tunes and lines bellow out to fabulously mixed audiences. This theatre company has a rare knack of perfectly presenting laidback performances that are a seamless mix of intelligent, educational, deeply moving and crisply funny. Mikron reels its audience in, rips tears from deep places and lays creases lightly on laughter-filled faces. Its performances are a compelling concoction of British eccentricity and social history, stirred into a frothy potion of canal charisma.

Mikron tells stories that reflect the mighty voices of ordinary people, and through art it preserves those intimate tales of important social history, that might otherwise be lost. Mikron offers the precious gift of accessible live theatre, with plays that are brilliant quaffable fun, yet yield deeply.

ABOVE: Mikron's cast for 'Can you keep a secret?' in 2012
(left to right) Caroline Hallam, Nicholas Coutu-Langmead, Ruth Cataroche, Robert Took

WHERE

Huddersfield Narrow Canal
Based in Marsden. OS SE045115
Mikron tour all summer in their narrowboat, Tyseley, and by road during the autumn. Their show schedule gives details of tour dates and which canalside locations they will be performing at during the season.

MORE INFO

Mikron acquired its current narrowboat Tyseley in 1975. Tyseley is listed on the National Register of Historic Vessels (NRHV) and was originally commissioned by the Grand Union Canal Carrying Company in 1937, later being converted into the first ever restaurant boat on the canals. Since Mikron has owned her, she has a new bottom and sides thanks to £50,000 raised for the work.

www.nationalhistoricships.org.uk

Mikron celebrated 40 years in 2012, and are always keen for new supporters. You can support them by going to see one of their shows, becoming a 'Friend of Mikron', sponsoring a show, buying merchandise from their online shop (including Mike Lucas' book about Mikron 'I'd go back tomorrow'), or just spreading the word...

www.mikron.org.uk

Visit our website for more about the 100 Treasures, and tell us your favourite treasure www.coolcanals.com/100treasures

18 COG
The bare roots of canal mechanics

The ultimate marvel of Britain's canals remains how still water manages to leap over hills, roll into valleys and tip into seas, defiantly clambering every ugly and beautiful crevice of our island's landscape. Boats have celebrated this for over 200 years, venturing inconceivably inland along these historic manmade trade routes - and canals have been hailed for their triumph over the challenge. Grand architectural and engineering exhibits deserve every trumpet blow that belts out, but often behind the razzmatazz the real hero remains unserenaded. The truth is that canals conquered Britain's contours because of one simple mechanism - the cog.

The living story of the canals began when James Brindley famously brought his ingenious plan of enabling boats without engines to climb uphill in still water and, behind Brindley's brilliance, the cog quietly became the Trojan of the canals.

Of course the cog has its own history, and before the first clod of earth was dug on Brindley's first canal, the cog was already changing the world in its own right, regardless of canals.

It was Archimedes, the Greek mathematician, who in his study of the orbit of planets first discovered the concept of the cog wheel. Then, in another cerebral era, Leonardo da Vinci experimented with rotary movement and the cog gear was born. He applied his genius to thoughts about pendulums, swinging, cranking and hoisting motion from the simple gear mechanism. The machine was born. Wind and water provided energy and the world had to prepare itself for the inevitability of an Industrial Revolution.

ABOVE: Lockkeeper at Bratch Locks on the Staffordshire & Worcestershire Canal, using a windlass to operate the lock

When the cog was first invented it was sculpted from wood, but later the solid steel cog forged its own future. The cog has played its part in everything from the bicycle and the car to the spinning wheel, the steam engine and Greenwich Mean Time. With simple magnificence the cog clunked beautifully with the rhythm of industry, and its well-oiled reliability helped make the tiniest watches and the heaviest machinery to fire the most potent ammunition of capitalism.

Iconic outstretched black and white lock arms steal the canal limelight, while the humble cog does the work. Solid, unassuming, lightly greased and silently ready for every traveller that passes through... Across the calm of the water, when the 'clonk,clink,clonk,clink...' starts winding, the waterways know someone is using the lock. This is the sound of water travel, holding the anticipation of every boater. The water won't be hurried by the windlass and it usually takes 10 minutes to fill and empty a lock. But in canal terms this is not just function and motion, it's a constitutional break, where time waits and passing strangers chat about the weather or more.

No one has needed to improve how a lock works under the power of the cog wheel, and progress hasn't

spoiled the pleasure of water travel. The simple small cog that stands at the four corners of a lock, waiting to lift the paddles, is our precious living heritage. Mini monuments in their own right, to be cherished with pride. Cogs are the sound, the sight and oily smell of the waterways. Ingenious simplicity, sculpturally beautiful, unarguably a treasure of Britain's canals.

WHERE
On canals throughout Britain
The canals are open all day every day - just find your local canal.

MORE INFO
The primary use of the cog on Britain's canals is of course the mechanism of the ubiquitous lock - turning the cogs with the help of the windlass is familiar to every boater. But there are cogs at work in boat engines, in steam rooms, and even the great pumping stations that kept the water circulating the canals use mighty cogs.

Visit our website for more about the 100 Treasures, and tell us your favourite treasure www.coolcanals.com/100treasures

19 FOXTON TRAIL
Narrowboats scrambling uphill

Foxton is a place to wallow in the sheer joy of the living heritage of Britain's canals. It's like an open-air museum, without stuffiness, counting boats in and out of its lock flight in the same way as it did when it opened in 1812. Visitors to Foxton can follow the fascinating Canal & River Trust trail (marked by arrows tiled on the ground and on posts) on an adventure that explores a site that is both historically intriguing and stunningly beautiful.

At the top of the lock flight, passersby bump into John Cryer, a life-sized model of the former lockkeeper. He will witter on, to anyone who'll listen, about his life as a lockkeeper in the old days when narrowboats rushed through, laden with sugar, tea, soap, tinned food, chemicals and paper. Anyone who overstays their welcome in John's company will hear the story again, and his rock hard, stone cold cup of tea will never empty.

The old stables next door to John's cottage, at the edge of the lock flight, have become a discovery room with displays about the 50-60 horses that once travelled through the locks every day. Following the trail, the locks lead downhill in a staircase flight with 10 locks that descend 75ft and use 25,000 gallons of water with every boat that travels through today. Boats need to book their journey time, and pass through in gluts with the assistance of the (living) lockkeeper. The route is a challenge for boaters and is always high drama to watch.

ABOVE: Entering Foxton Staircase Locks

The waymarked trail twists to the other side of the hill, where the remains of Foxton Inclined Plane lie. Old rail tracks cling into the grassy hill, tantalisingly almost intact, running from the canal at the bottom of the hill to the canal at the higher level. In 1900 the inclined plane was opened to bypass Foxton Locks, saving almost an hour on a boat's journey time. Narrowboats were lifted sideways, in two caissons (water-holding tanks). The caissons were hauled up hill by a cable and a steam-driven winch. The madness of tugging a narrowboat up a dry hill is simply thrilling to imagine from a windswept viewpoint over some rubble on a hillside.

Foxton Trail has an award-winning recently renovated museum, outdoor exhibits, historic buildings, boat trips, pubs, teashops, ice-creams and an exuberant landscape with uplifting views over the best Leicestershire landscape: a glorious canal experience and a perfect day out.

ABOVE: The remnants of Foxton Inclined Plane overlooking Leicestershire countryside

LOCATION

Grand Union Canal - Leicester Section
Foxton. OS SP691897
The entire Foxton site is open all day every day. FREE admission (there's a small charge for the car park). Audio trail.

Foxton Canal Museum
Open daily throughout the summer. Winter weekends only (weekday visits can be arranged). Gift shop. Small admission charge. Wheelchair access. Run by the Foxton Inclined Plane Trust.

MORE INFO

Day boats & boat trips www.foxtonboats.co.uk

Foxton Inclined Plane is a Scheduled Ancient Monument and Foxton Locks are Grade II*-listed. The Lockkeeper's cottage by Top Lock and Lockkeeper's cottage, stable block & craft shop by Bottom Lock are all Grade II-listed. The Inclined Plane and the Staircase Locks have both been awarded Transport Trust Red Wheel Plaques.

www.transporttrust.com www.transportheritage.com

Foxton Inclined Plane was abandoned after only 10 years of use because it cost too much to keep in operation. Foxton Inclined Plane Trust are behind a restoration project that hopes to reopen the plane one day.

T:01162 792657 www.fipt.org.uk

20 BRISTOL FLOATING HARBOUR
Keeping ships afloat

Bristol is a city of push bikes and boats, it's home to Wallace and Gromit, Banksy and buskers in sandals with tin whistles. The ethos of the modern Bristolian rides a skyline that unapologetically washes old and new together. Architecture tells its own stories and the Floating Harbour wafts the strongest flavours of the past and present in the showcase of the city.

Cobblestones and cars on the harbourside create comforting patterns of eras gone and yet to come, while distant seagulls and seashells tease tourists with faraway thoughts. This is a travellers' city, simmering with stories of explorers, immigrants and migrants.

A life-sized sculpture of John Cabot (1425-1500) has his salt-weathered face peering towards the sea that he once journeyed to 'discover' North America, and claim it for England.

Bristol's relationship with the sea has been a constant battle with the tides, and its importance as a port is surprising given all the odds nature threw against it. Before the Floating Harbour was built, the Mud Dock which dates back to 1625 was the wretched place where ships once had to berth on the soft muddy bottom of the river. The tides of Bristol's two rivers played havoc with the moored ships, whose crews had to tidy away spars and rigging in a bid to reduce damage as the tides fell. "All shipshape and Bristol fashion!" is the phrase that carries the cries of those crews.

In 1802 William Jessop was given the task of making plans for a harbour that would create safer moorings with ships being kept afloat instead of stranded in mud (hence the name Floating Harbour). The harbour opened several years later and the port prospered during the Industrial Revolution, becoming Britain's second major transatlantic port after Liverpool. Bristol's prosperity came from boats arriving with tobacco, rum, cotton, timber and sugar; and leaving with finished cotton goods, glass, brassware and soap. Tragically, the revolting truth of the slave trade festers in Bristol's darkest history. Around 40 per cent of the city's income was connected to the slave trade by 1740.

ABOVE: The stone tower was originally the base for a steam crane, which was scrapped in 1969

With its heritage blustering with gloom and glory, the Bristolian spirit is captured in the Floating Harbour today. This is a tourist destination layered with contemporary art galleries, trendy eating, cutting-edge museums, narrowboats (dwarfed by giant ships) bobbing in the water, cranes and sculptures and everything a leisure seeker needs for 'A Grand Day Out'.

ABOVE: Along the harbourside with the Museum of Bristol across the water

WHERE
Kennet & Avon Canal
Bristol. OS ST585723
The Floating Harbour is open all day every day.

MORE INFO
Former historic warehouses and transit sheds now house art galleries including the Arnolfini, the Museum of Bristol (in the M Shed), the Watershed Media Centre (in the E & W Sheds).

An online resource of information, historical documents and photographs of Bristol's Floating Harbour

www.bristolfloatingharbour.org.uk   www.mshed.org   www.shipshapebristol.co.uk

Bristol Harbour Festival is Bristol's biggest cultural festival and one of the largest FREE festivals in the UK. Held in July.

www.bristolharbourfestival.co.uk

Bristol Tourist Info www.visitbristol.co.uk

Visit our website for more about the 100 Treasures, and tell us your favourite treasure www.coolcanals.com/100treasures

My favourite treasures - chosen and written by Nigel Crowe:
Head of Heritage for the Canal & River Trust

" Horses were vital to canals until powered boats arrived, and they required careful looking after.

Canal companies and carriers built stables at wharves, docks and boatyards, and at intervals, often linked to lock flights, along the line of a canal. Some of these stables were simple, open-sided sheds; others were more elaborate and more durable. 18th-century stables could be small and dirty, but from the early 19th century onwards company bylaws and commercial pressures led to higher standards. Most surviving canal stables date from the late 19th to early 20th century and are brick or stone built with small windows, 'stable doors' and pitched roofs, sometimes incorporating a hayloft.

Canal stables varied in size; some were large, many were quite small, typically with stalls for two to six horses. Inside, the floor was cobbled or setted or brick-lined, with a central drain and individual wooden stalls with hayracks and mangers.

Despite falling out of use, canal stables still survive today; good examples are found on the Birmingham Canal Navigations, Oxford, Grand Union, Leeds & Liverpool and Shropshire Union Canals. The stable block at Bunbury Locks on the Shropshire Union had stalls for 22 horses and a forage store. It stands right on the lock-side, which meant that horses could be unhitched from their tow-ropes and led straight inside. There is a similar block at Delph Locks on the Dudley No 1 Canal. In recognition of their special historic interest, both these stables are listed buildings.

One stable block that can easily be visited is that at the National Waterways Museum in Ellesmere Port. This has a cobbled floor and individual stalls and mangers for horses. It was restored by volunteers in the 1970s and gives a very good idea of what these once common canalside buildings were really like. **"**
NIGEL CROWE

WHERE
On canals throughout Britain
The canals are open all day every day - just find your local canal. The stable block in the National Waterways Museum at Ellesmere Port has displays of horse-related paraphernalia.

www.nwm.org.uk

MORE INFO
The Horseboating Society works to promote horseboating and preserve its heritage and skills. www.horseboating.org.uk

Working horses, mules and donkeys in some of the poorest countries of the world can suffer unnecessary hardships. The Brooke is a charity that aims to improve the lives and welfare of these working animals. www.thebrooke.org

Visit our website for more about the 100 Treasures, and tell us your favourite treasure www.coolcanals.com/100treasures

RIGHT: Inside the stable block at the National Waterways Museum in Ellesmere Port

22 STANDEDGE TUNNEL
Burrowing through the Pennines

The Pennines hug the sky with an obstinacy that forbids anyone except the hardiest scrambler to pass - and when the first canal builders arrived, the obstacle loomed down with cold screams of an impossible route. But the bulldog jaws of Canal Mania weren't going to let man, nor beast, stand in the way - so navvies, armed with shovels, knuckled onwards, gobbling straight through the backbone of Britain. A tunnel was built and those brave navvies leave their legacy for a nation to cherish. Theirs is a story to respect, and Standedge Tunnel has become one of Britain's best treasures to marvel over, one of the wonders of the waterways.

ABOVE: Pennine moors

Standedge Tunnel is the longest, highest and deepest tunnel on Britain's inland waterways, charging 3¼ miles (5,029m) from one side of the Pennines at Marsden to Diggle at the other. Work on the Huddersfield Narrow Canal began in 1794, with a shockingly brave route that planned to burrow under the Pennines. There was bound to be trouble ahead when two teams of navvies began hacking the tunnel from either end. A blunder was blooming with every shovelful removed, as the team at the Diggle end were unwittingly progressing several feet higher than those at the Marsden end.

The Pennines weren't going to submit easily and the project was plagued with errors. Attempts to correct the mistakes only led to several collapses in the tunnel and water seeping through. If blame was to be cast, it was aimed at Benjamin Outram who was the official canal engineer commissioned for the job, but he was a busy engineer and had left much of the supervision to the less experienced surveyor, Nicholas Brown. To add to the burdens of the mismanaged canal build, the floods of 1799 washed away sections of the canal. Outram resigned and the canal hero, Telford, was consulted to complete the tunnel.

Now the tunnel cut through the hard millstone grit of Marston Moor with the ease of Thomas Telford's own grit and brilliance. By 1811 the tunnel was open for business and the previously disconnected Huddersfield Narrow Canal had become a through route at last.

To save money, the tunnel had been built without towpaths, leaving boat horses to trot over the moors above while boat crews were cursed with the gruelling task of legging through the bowels of the earth. Boatmen had to lie on their backs on top of their boats and walk their laden boats through the darkness, pushing with boots along the low arched brickwork that lined the tunnel. Some parts were unlined, and the rock face would have menaced tired leggers, but endurance was vital as wages depended on the speedy carriage of cargo loaded on their boats. In the heyday of Canal Mania, the route became ludicrously busy - and crews were put under increasing pressure to deliver their goods on time. Since the tunnel only fitted one boat width, fights inevitably broke out when boats met and both crews refused to back up.

The canal company stepped in and only allowed its official leggers to operate in the tunnels. Traffic congestion was controlled with a one way rule on a 4-hourly rota each way. Britain's canal boats were forced to do what Britain does best, and queue! Boats politely lined up outside the tunnel for their turn. Equilibrium was restored with the new leggers who lived in the Tunnel End Cottages and earned a shilling for their trouble each trip. The tunnel could have been set to live happily ever after if the Huddersfield and

Manchester Railway Company hadn't bought the canal and its tunnel. A railway line was built to follow a similar route and the canal was doomed. The last commercial boat travelled through the tunnel in 1921 and the canal was finally closed in 1944.

The fairy-tale ending had to wait for another generation of canal enthusiasm. And in 2001, on May 1st, HRH Prince Charles turned up to cheering crowds. After a 20-year restoration programme, the tunnel and the Huddersfield Narrow Canal were open for boats again.

WHERE

Huddersfield Narrow Canal
Marsden. OS SE040119
Open Mar-Nov Tues-Sun. Closed Mon except School and Bank holidays. Café and gift shop. Entry FREE to Visitor Centre, grounds, café & gift shop. Boat Trips (charge). Wheelchair access. Disabled access to glass-roofed boat trips and Visitor Centre but no access on the through-tunnel trip. Discount for Friends of the Canal & River Trust.

MORE INFO

Boat Trip - 30-minute passenger boat trips into the tunnel, in glass-roofed boats with a specialist guide. 3-hr through boat trip is only available 1st Sat of the month.

The Pennine Way crosses the moors above Standedge Tunnel. The entrance portal at Tunnel End is Grade II*-listed, and Standedge Tunnel has been awarded a Transport Trust Red Wheel Plaque.

www.transporttrust.com www.transportheritage.com

T:01484 844298 www.standedge.co.uk

Visit our website for more about the 100 Treasures, and tell us your favourite treasure www.coolcanals.com/100treasures

23 MUTE SWAN
Royalty and grace

They are the giant souls of the waterways, with the grace of angels and the spirit of fire. Swans stir something in the human psyche that heightens the emotions - irresistible to poets, painters, composers and ballerinas. Mute swans might hiss or bark under stress, but take time to look with gentle care into the eye of a swan and a unique, individual character will talk silently back.

Sublime beauty is a decoy to the commanding role swans play along the canals. This big white-feathered creature is happy to mingle on the water with moorhens, ducks, coots and herons, but everyone knows to keep a peck or a grunt away from these majestic beasts when they are told to. We humans can tuck into a

ABOVE: Proudly guarding his territory

Sunday dinner of goose or duck if we want to, but a plateful of swan would be treason. Swans have Royal status. Her Majesty The Queen still claims her ownership of swans, although these days that usually only applies on certain sections of the Thames.

Ever since the Middle Ages, it has been the Royal Swan Master's job to organise the annual swan upping. The event today is mostly ceremonial, but it still has purpose as a swan census. On specific sections of the River Thames, Royal Swan Uppers don scarlet red jackets and round up the swans on the water. Unmarked swans are identified with their parentage and then marked before being returned to the wild.

During the mid-1980s there was a serious decline in the swan population and fishermen's lead weights were banned (replaced with a non-toxic equivalent) in a bid to help protect swans from pollution. Boat users and anglers are on the increase in recent years and they, as well as organisations such as the RSPCA, RSPB, The Swan Sanctuary and the Queen's Swan Marker, are all responsible for helping to protect the swans from pollution and vandalism.

The spring scene of two swans with their brood of fluffy feathered cygnets sploshing in water is a sight to treasure. The hope of another generation of swans is held in each fragile nest across the waterways.

An anthrometamorphic idyll loves the notion of swans mating for life, but in reality swans have an average of 4 mates over a lifetime. No matter what the swan divorce rate is, it doesn't take an expert to grasp that they display phenomenal parenting skills. Their shared role looking after their cygnets is touching to see.

Swans emit simplicity and majesty in an aura that somehow reflects the waterways they inhabit. They symbolise power and strength, heritage and beauty, nurturing and regeneration - a living treasure of immense gravitas.

ABOVE: Swans are dedicated parents

WHERE
On canals throughout Britain
The canals are open all day every day - just find your local canal. Spring is of course the best time to see new cygnets.

MORE INFO
The Royal Swan Upping on the Thames takes place towards the end of July each year.

www.royalswan.co.uk

CAMRA (Campaign for Real Ale) claims the Swan is the 4th most common pub name in the UK. One of many theories why so many historic pubs have the name is that Henry VIII's wife, Anne of Cleeves, had a white swan as her family crest and pubs adopted the name in respect for her. For obvious reasons, many pubs along the canals are named the Swan.

www.camra.org.uk   www.pubisthehub.org.uk   www.coolcanals.com (Full listings of all canalside pubs in Britain)

A swan's wingspan can be up to 8ft and in flight they can reach a speed of up to 55mph.

www.theswansanctuary.org.uk

Visit our website for more about the 100 Treasures, and tell us your favourite treasure www.coolcanals.com/100treasures

TELFORD'S PLANS
The work of one of Scotland's most cherished celebrities

On August 9th 1757, in a remote Scottish dale, a shepherd and his wife had a baby boy. They called him Thomas. After a lifetime of enormous achievements, when their son died, aged 77, he was buried with the tears of a nation and all honours in Westminster Abbey. Thomas Telford was the Scottish civil engineer who, through his work, had earned the right to be immortalised in public statues, have a town named after him, and be a household name for over 200 years.

His genius was a gift, but his early career wasn't paved by wealth or society connections. Telford's father died before he had time to know him, and as a small boy he was destined to work hard, taking over the family role of shepherd. Education introduced him to science and art and when he was 14 he chose to be an apprentice to a stonemason. In 1780 he went to Edinburgh and in 1782 to London.

ABOVE: Thomas Telford (National Waterways Archive)

By 1793 his talent was under the spotlight and he was asked to work on the Ellesmere Canal with Jessop, another great canal engineer. Telford became the giant amongst all the amazing engineers of his era, and his work has stunned every generation since. Pontcysyllte Aqueduct, completed in 1805, still shakes the world with its herculean structure; and Telford's fame lives on in other spectacular achievements such as the road from London to Holyhead with the 579ft span wrought-iron Menai Suspension Bridge (1819-26), St Katherine's Docks (1824-28) in London, and the unbelievable coast to coast Caledonian Canal (completed in 1822) in the Scottish Highlands.

Before the construction of any project could begin, Telford had to draw plans for his team to follow. Before the age of computers, every plan was hand drawn, and handed to others, to miraculously turn a plan into a structure. Some of his plans have survived and those marks made direct from his hand present a thrilling connection with the man behind the marvels he built.

Telford never married and he was dedicated to his craft. He helped to found the Institution of Civil Engineers in 1818 giving the profession status it still nurtures today. But his influence wasn't only contained within his work. He was a likeable man, who inspired others through his cheery demeanour, and the boy who started life herding sheep, grew into the man people wanted to follow.

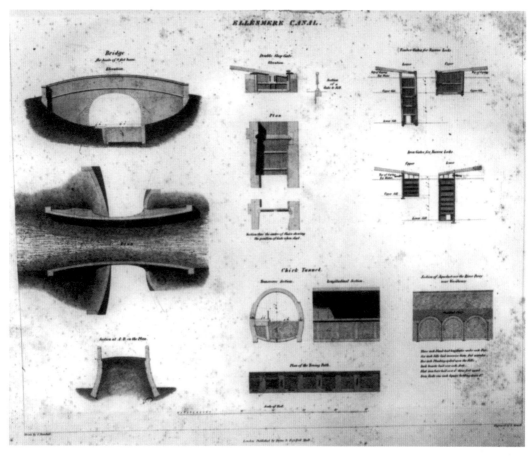

ABOVE: Historic plans for the Ellesmere Canal kept in the National Waterways Archive

WHERE

On canals throughout Britain
The canals are open all day every day - just find your local canal. Telford's magnificent engineering works can be seen throughout Britain, from the Pontcysyllte Aqueduct in Wales, to Neptune's Staircase in Scotland and St Katherine's Docks in London.

Plans drawn up by Thomas Telford are kept in the National Waterways Archive in the National Waterways Museum at Ellesmere Port. Access to the Archive is FREE but must be prebooked.

T:0151 3555017 www.nwm.org.uk

MORE INFO

Thomas Telford was the first President of the Institution of Civil Engineers, set up in 1818, and remained so until his death in 1834. The Institution's commercial arm is even called Thomas Telford Ltd today.

www.ice.org.uk

Visit our website for more about the 100 Treasures, and tell us your favourite treasure www.coolcanals.com/100treasures

My favourite treasures - chosen and written by Nigel Crowe:
Head of Heritage for the Canal & River Trust

Bollards are the poor man's sculpture of the waterways. They occur at locksides, landings, wharves, basins and docks and come in a variety of shapes, sizes and materials.

The earliest bollards have all disappeared but later wood, stone, cast iron and concrete examples abound. Canal companies often favoured a distinctive style: fat bulbs on the Grand Union, plain phalluses on the Birmingham Canal Navigations. Elsewhere there are anonymous dollies, mushrooms and stumps and more rarely, the occasional inverted cone. These humble objects lend character to many canalscapes.

Dozens of white-painted bollards dot the windswept banks of the Gloucester & Sharpness Canal (like notes in a musical score) and there are still ancient wooden stumps with whitened tops to be found on rural Midlands canals.

Bollard-fanciers can find cracking examples at Liverpool Docks and around the lesser known basin at Bridgwater Dock, which is approached along the Bridgwater & Taunton Canal's towpath after passing through the unforgettable Albert Street cutting. **"**
NIGEL CROWE

LEFT: The black & white of a typical mooring bollard on the Worcester & Birmingham Canal

WHERE
On canals throughout Britain

MORE INFO
The canals are open all day every day - just find your local canal.

Visit our website for more about the 100 Treasures, and tell us your favourite treasure www.coolcanals.com/100treasures

RIGHT: One of the huge mooring bollards on the Gloucester & Sharpness Canal

26 PRESIDENT
Britain's last steam-powered narrowboat

Steam engines and riveted wrought iron might seem the stuff of beautifully solid Fred Dibnah-style men, but most historic canal boats have a canny way of defying class and gender when they suck anyone who visits them into their web of intrigue. President is a unique steam-powered narrowboat, built in 1909 by the famous company Fellows, Morton and Clayton at Saltley in Birmingham. She's a floating statement of power, beauty and nostalgia, and an experience that means something to everyone.

When she was first built she cost £600, now she is the priceless treasure owned by the Black Country Living Museum. The museum and the voluntary help of the Friends of President care for and operate the boat which tours the canals and appears at many of the waterways festivals and events every year.

ABOVE: President and Kildare lying at the Black Country Living Museum, as if time had stood still since the Industrial Revolution

In her early years she carried foodstuffs, tea, sugar and flour on the canals between London and the Midlands. Her steam engine puffed tirelessly day and night as crews changed on a rota to keep the boat running to tight delivery schedules. Inside the tiny boatman's cabin the bed was scarcely needed, and the kettle a mere distraction from the task of the crew. The burly business of haulage, past and present, doesn't necessarily covet fashion or frills, but narrowboats can't help but own grace and beauty.

President has always commanded respect and the changing times that meddled with her structure have only added to her colourful story. President's specially developed compound steam engine and coke-fired boiler took up a huge area in the hull that was needed for cargo, but in its time it competed well with horse-drawn boats. Steamers could only carry around 18 tons and a horse could manage over 25 tons. The advantage steamers had was that they were powerful enough to tow several butty boats (unpowered boats). So, although steamers were flawed by the cumbersome size of the engine and its boiler, they introduced a new concept of speed and insisted the manmade engine was here to stay.

Eventually a magnificent Bolinder engine replaced President's steam engine. With its new 15hp engine tucked into a much smaller space, President could carry more cargo for the business she was built for. By 1925 she was cruising the canals with the new colours of red, yellow and green, in 1946 she was sold, and later changed hands again to carry coal. Her swansong was her time with British Waterways northern maintenance fleet at Northwich working on the Trent & Mersey, Macclesfield and Shropshire Union Canals. Then finally President retired.

ABOVE: President and her butty boat Kildare attracting attention at a waterways festival

Her time had been served and she aged without purpose, until she was finally sold in 1973, as no more than a derelict hull. A valiant effort led to her restoration and, with meticulous attention, dedication and passion, her boatman's cabin was refitted and she was graced with a glorious steam engine that gave her power again. President was back and the eyes of the world came to admire her. When she's not out and about showing off, she can be found proudly resting together with her butty Kildare at their base at the Black Country Living Museum.

WHERE
President can be seen at the Black Country Living Museum or at waterways festivals and events throughout the year

MORE INFO
There is always an opportunity to see President and her butty Kildare and ask the crew members more about them. Alternatively you could become a volunteer crew member - familiarisation days are held to run through the specific needs of the boat, and crews are needed to move the boats around the networks.

For President's full itinerary, visit the website. President is looked after by volunteers, the Friends of President, who are always looking for new members.

President is listed on the National Register of Historic Vessels (NRHV), and was given the honour in 2012 of taking part in the Thames Diamond Jubilee Pageant in London in celebration of Her Majesty The Queen's 60-year reign.

www.nationalhistoricships.org.uk

Friends of President www.nb-president.org.uk

27 STRATFORD'S CANAL
The Shakespearian trail

My favourite treasure - chosen by Tony Hales MBE:
Chairman of British Waterways and the Canal & River Trust.
"My ultimate favourite is the Stratford Canal near my home. It is my haven of peace and tranquility and is filled with memories of gentle family walks or at a faster pace just with Caspar, our dog. Starting my walk at England's longest aqueduct at Edstone and crossing two more smaller cast iron ones, the canal gently winds its way through the heart of England's countryside and has three charming and friendly pubs all serving decent food and beer on route. A unique feature of the canal is the barrel roofed cottages alongside, that fit perfectly with the curves of the little bridges crossing the canal... it's my home and my peace and that's why I love it."

When summer arrives, the picture of people lazing on the grassy waterside in Stratford Basin is one of England's best. The Royal Shakespeare Theatre watches over the gangs of geese and ducks, while the Baguette Barge and the ice-cream boat tempt sunbathers. Stratford-upon-Avon is the second most visited tourist destination in Britain after London. And while tourists crowd over kitsch Shakespearian souvenirs and plastic models of the Queen, the canal strolls along the edge of town.

The matching black and white colours of the canal's lock arms melt into an Elizabethan landscape, next to swaying willow trees and charming split bridges that cross the water. There are three aqueducts on the Stratford-upon-Avon Canal that might, at first glance, seem quite ordinary; but the twist in the tale of this trio is kept exclusively for those who visit. These three quirky aqueducts prove that not every engineering structure has to soar as high as eagles or be ornate in design to thrill the canal traveller. The Edstone Aqueduct (sometimes known as Bearley Aqueduct because of the nearby village of the same name) is the largest of the Stratford three, and at 250 yards is the longest in England. It was built in the 1800s, not far from Mary Arden's house (Shakespeare's mother) at Wilmcote, only one and a half miles south of Edstone at bridge 59. The cast-iron trough is held up by 13 brick pillars as it strides over an unspectacular shallow valley. The towpath traveller's approach is no more than pleasant, but on crossing the aqueduct the intrigue brims over as the towpath hugs the water at a different level to other aqueducts around the canal networks. The walker's feet are level with the bottom of the tank, giving a quirky duck's eye view of the water. When a narrowboat passes by, the excitement is ridiculous.

Don't let Shakespeare, or the shocking number of tourists who turn up in Stratford every day fool you

ABOVE: Cottage by Lowsonford Lock - engineers building the Stratford Canal knew more about building bridges than houses, so when they had to build lock cottages, they adapted their skills resulting in the distinctive barrel-shaped roof

- Stratford is more than just a shrine to Shakespeare. Its streets are lined with Victorian lamp posts and living oaks that stood here before the bard was born. The bard's hometown has aged into a magnificently overblown symbol of English zest. It's an every-day festival of Englishness, a place folk flock to go sightseeing or shopping, or even to go to the theatre. The canal hadn't arrived in Stratford in Shakespeare's time, but if he was a tourist today he'd probably head for the canal basin to laze at the water's edge, and he'd definitely have a few words to say about it.

LOCATION

Stratford-upon-Avon Canal
Stratford-upon-Avon. OS SP204548
The entire canal is open all day every day. There are no barriers or admission charges - just visit at any time.

MORE INFO

The Stratford Canal meets the river Avon in Bancroft Basin. It's a honeypot site for tourists from across the world visiting the Royal Shakespeare Theatre which overlooks the river there. The theatre is home to the Royal Shakespeare Company (RSC), one of the world's best-known theatre companies. www.rsc.org.uk

The canal runs through Wilmcote, where the Shakespeare Birthplace Trust run Shakespeare's mother's former home as an authentic Tudor farm. Mary Arden's Farm is a short walk from the canal. www.shakespeare.org.uk

All thee aqueducts on the Stratford Canal - Edstone, Wootton Wawen and Yarningale - are Grade II*-listed.

www.shakespeare-country.co.uk

Visit our website for more about the 100 Treasures, and tell us your favourite treasure www.coolcanals.com/100treasures

Brindley, Telford, Jessop and all the greatest engineers of an era couldn't have built their canals just for the thrill of it. It was world markets and entrepreneurs that created the demand and funding for the canals. Men such as Wedgwood and Cadbury drove dynasties that defined regions on the map of Britain. And, in turn, a region's industry shaped its landscape, perfumed its air and bred skills and traditions into generations of working families. Geography and people are bound by the trades that nurtured a nation's heritage.

An area just north of the Midlands and south of 'the North' became known as The Potteries. Stoke-on-Trent exploded onto a stretch of land, building a pottery industry that knew no bounds. The city's heritage rattles with pots, and its population grew up on patterns of blue willow and glaze-fired fumes.

When the pottery industry first began, fragile pots had to be transported laboriously over rugged tracks by packhorse, but mass production needed canalboats to carry its cargo. In 1777 James Brindley built the Trent & Mersey Canal to link the 'Potteries' to the world and British designs and manufacturing processes boomed in Victorian times.

After over 200 years of changes, and the devastating economic recession of recent times, Britain's traditional pottery industry has been left struggling to survive. As potteries closed, Stoke-on-Trent's silhouette cracked with unemployment and generations of skills were wasted. In the 1900s there were around 2,000 bottle ovens shaping the skyline of Stoke-on-Trent, now only 46 remain. Middleport Pottery is a survivor, and home to the largest standing bottle oven. It also contains the largest mould collection in Europe with over 19,000 dating back 150 years. This pottery has battled against changing times by creatively operating as both a working factory and a visitor attraction. It is a triumph of preservation, with simple old-fashioned open fires and factory ambience to boost its appeal in modern times.

Middleport Pottery is the only place in the world that still uses a 200-year-old decorating technique that a skilled worker can only perfect after around seven years of training. Middleport, the home of Burleighware, is a factory making the world-famous blue and white floral tableware which has been manufactured here since 1888. Traditional methods are cherished here, with patterns still printed on tissue by hand-engraved copper rollers, and rubbed onto pots. The famous Willow patterns are still lovingly fired before being glazed and fired a third time to ensure its ink won't fade. Good old-fashioned labour intensive methods are something Middleport has managed to harness in its business model, and it is with pride that the pottery tells its customers that 'at least 25 members of staff have worked on each product from clay to finish'. The factory shop can show off about selling pots that are 'refreshingly unique in an era of mass production'.

In 2009 Middleport screamed out for help when it was in danger of closure. It was the last working Victorian pottery in the country using traditional manufacturing techniques. The Prince's Regeneration Trust came to the rescue, acquiring the site in 2011 and steering a £7.5million project to save its Grade II-listed buildings and priceless Victorian skills. Quite rightly, this pottery attracts excitement - English Heritage has described Middleport as 'a national treasure', and Stoke-on-Trent hit the streets with flags and faces when HRH Prince Charles turned up to visit the factory. But more important than the razzmatazz, is the recognition that this historic factory is where traditional English pottery skills must be handed on to another generation - an extraordinary factory that passes on extraordinary skills under the everyday chatter of its proud workforce.

ABOVE: Middleport Pottery's huge building overlooks the Trent & Mersey Canal

WHERE

Trent & Mersey Canal
Stoke-on-Trent. OS SJ859495
The Burleigh Factory Shop is open daily. All Burleighware is handmade in Middleport Pottery, and the shop has the largest selection of Burleighware anywhere in the world.

www.burleigh.co.uk

MORE INFO

Middleport Pottery is the last working Victorian pottery in Britain, and still uses original machinery (such as the Boulton steam engine installed in 1888). The Pottery is Grade II*-listed.

The project to regenerate the entire Middleport site, aims to save not only the pottery, but also create a new craft hub. As work progresses, it will be possible to visit other parts of the site with organised tours. The Pottery will keep working throughout the process.

The Prince's Regeneration Trust www.princes-regeneration.org

T:020 3262 0560 www.middleportpottery.co.uk

Visit our website for more about the 100 Treasures, and tell us your favourite treasure www.coolcanals.com/100treasures

29

CANALSIDE INN
The heart of the canal community

Canalside pubs and inns are the bricks and mortar of canal heritage and, at the same time, the beating heart of today's canal community. It's the place where boaters gather at the end of a day cruising, a watering hole for cyclists, a chance for walkers to pull off their boots and take time over lunch, a meeting place for landlubbing locals and a vital hub for an entire canal community.

Oddly, even before the canals were built, pubs were at the centre of canal life. Meetings between engineers, financiers, landowners and other parties interested in the arrival of new canals would often take place in the meeting rooms of an inn. And when their project was approved by an Act of Parliament, the canal companies could begin building the canal, and then build more pubs all along the routes for navvies and boatmen to use.

"Historically, canal pubs came in all shapes and sizes. A few were rough hovels serving rough ale, others were characterful farmhouse kitchen types and some were busy inns with wharfage, accommodation and stables. These inns were usually purpose-built to serve their waterway and often formed the focal point of a settlement. There are good examples at Hawkesbury Junction (Oxford & Coventry Canals), Honeystreet (Kennet & Avon Canal), Braunston and Stoke Bruerne (Grand Union Canal), and Garthmyl (Montgomery Canal). Others can be found standing at canal junctions or alongside lock flights like the Three Locks at Soulbury on the Grand Union Canal.

It is fascinating to discover through old photographs how canal inns have changed over the years. In the 1950s many still looked the same as they had in the 1890s when they were frequented by working boatmen. Modern demands have led to changes involving facelifts, extensions and redesigned interiors. Sometimes only the name remains unaltered although old-fashioned examples like the Spotted Dog, the Mermaid and the Sun, Moon and Stars are no longer common. Simple names like the Boat, the Anchor, the Swan, the Wharf Inn and the prosaic Canal Tavern are more popular now. Today's canal inns attract visitors to the waterways out of their cars as well as serving thirsty walkers, cyclists and boaters." Nigel Crowe, Head of Heritage Canal & River Trust, 2012

Canal pubs today seamlessly harbour shoulder-rubbing where differences (that might matter more in another parallel world) are diluted by the balm of canals. For over 200 years the canal pub has served boaters and adventurers, and passing strangers are always welcome. Bar stools that wobble on flagstone floors have propped generations of tales, and the secrets of the waterways still hug around the real fires, real ale and real atmosphere of a waterside pub.

The cheeks of the water traveller are kept rosy in summer with long lazy days gongoozling from a beer garden, and in winter huddled around a cosy open fire in the bar. Almost anywhere along the canals of Britain, at any time of year, the genuine welcome from licensees of canalside pubs can dazzle us with the warmest living heritage of all. An essential treasure of Britain's canals.

WHERE
On canals throughout Britain
The canals are open all day every day - just find your local canal.

MORE INFO
Full listings of all canalside inns in Britain can be found in our online directory. www.coolcanals.com

Visit our website for more about the 100 Treasures, and tell us your favourite treasure www.coolcanals.com/100treasures

RIGHT: The Barge Inn at Honeystreet on the Kennet & Avon Canal

30

HOLIDAY HIREBOAT
Colours of the canals

Untying the ropes and drifting away in a narrowboat is the dream holiday to leave the stress of daily life behind. The appeal is the tranquillity of waking with the ducks, and unhurried travel, with the journey in mind rather than a destination; then taking charge of a tiller and handling the ropes is a rugged enough challenge to spice the peace of it all. Holiday hireboat centres are based all around the navigable waterways, providing a leisure service without which canals would be a lesser place.

Canals weren't built for pleasure boats; 200 years ago they were the domain of the brutish business of haulage. The first canal boats to carry people rather than goods were packet boats on the Bridgewater Canal, but their purpose was not leisure, it was as a transport service that preceded the railways. When railways eventually arrived, they stole the Victorian heart and, in a bid to keep business, some canal companies tried offering a special speedy boat passenger service on boats called swifts. Galloping teams of horse-pulled

boats for what must have been a dynamic, if not frightening, experience. Needless to say, the railways had their way and the passenger transport business abandoned the canals along with commercial trade.

Canals were trapped with their image of being the filthy, and then unwanted, trade routes of the Industrial Revolution. Nobody thought of a holiday on the canals, even though the concept of messing about in boats on the river was becoming increasingly popular.

The British Waterways Board (later to become British Waterways, and now the Canal & River Trust) saw the need to attract new traffic to the canals if they were to stay alive, and a new mood was sweeping the waterways. Tom Rolt set off on a journey around the networks in his narrowboat called Cressy. He recorded the journey in his famous book 'Narrowboat' and a pioneering movement of canal enthusiasm was building momentum in the post-World War II years. Leisure boats were demanding their right to roam, and there was passionate outcry with every canal that was threatened with closure.

Struggling canal companies realised there might be a market for leisure craft now that the working boats had retired. Some companies adapted their fleets and canal tourism was dipping its toes into a new era. Small family-run hireboat companies launched, such as Canal Cruising Company in Stone near Stoke-on-Trent. The hippy 1970s flew by and by the 1980s many of the hireboat companies that the canals know now were established. They took their narrowboats to canals that reached into forgotten water roads rambling the Pennines, the Peak District, Welsh mountains, the Heart of England and now, thanks to the magnificent restoration and regeneration of canals over recent years, there's scarcely anywhere out of bounds for the adventurous holiday traveller.

The narrowboat for holiday hire bears everything and nothing in common with the traditional working boat of 200 years ago. A working boat family would have crammed into a small cabin at the stern while the cargo they carried filled the main space. The modern narrowboat looks deliciously similar on the outside, but

ABOVE: Boat dog in action at Hatton Locks on the Grand Union Canal

inside is a 'Tardis' of luxury with every mod con a happy tourist expects: shower, TV, cushions and plug-in convenience. Some companies, such as Moonraker specialise with high-end boats even offering the full fuss and frills, and unapologetic decadence, of an onboard Jacuzzi.

Each company has its own colours that cruise far and wide. Holiday hireboats have become the big colours of the canals and people come from all across the world to go on the holiday of a lifetime on a canal boat. Hireboat companies are part of the success story of Britain's canals.

WHERE
On canals throughout Britain
The canals are open all day every day - just find your local canal.

MORE INFO
Full listings of all canal holiday hireboat companies in Britain can be found in our online directory.

www.coolcanals.com

Visit our website for more about the 100 Treasures, and tell us your favourite treasure www.coolcanals.com/100treasures

A museum, by definition, is meant to be a building where objects of interest are stored and exhibited, but the National Waterways Museum is a magnificent rebel. Its buildings are part of the whole show, and no matter where the eye spins, indoors or outdoors, there's always something extraordinary to see.

The museum is housed in the old wharf, built in 1844 for the region's canal system. Canal engineers Thomas Telford and William Jessop had the task of linking Ellesmere with the Mersey and Liverpool (which was the biggest port in the world at that time). As Ellesmere Port thrived, magnificent warehouses were built to store china, bone and lime, and a dry dock served the boats that did business here. Despite the energetic years of success, progress was bound to have its own way and business eventually abandoned the canals, forcing the doomed site to close in the 1960s.

In the 1970s, five dedicated volunteers, in their mission to help preserve the traditions and history of the inland waterways, set out to give Ellesmere Port new life. They made the place home to an unprecedented collection of historic boats that were lovingly restored and protected. Their skill for protecting waterways heritage planted firm roots for developments that led to the museum that exists today. In 2000 the Waterways Trust took on the care of the museum and since 2012, in a new partnership, it is now cared for by the Canal & River Trust.

There are artefacts galore and spectacular events and exhibitions throughout the year, but the real heroes of the museum today must be the historic boats that bob up and down on the water. Some come and go, and some live full-time at the museum, lying unceremoniously in typical no-fuss canal style. Wide boats, narrow boats, tugs, ice-breakers, everything from the tiniest mine boat that was used to carry coal on the first canal in Britain, to the dramatic Clyde Puffer of the Scottish canals. A staggering collection of boats past and present pull at the heart strings as they call from the water for attention. Some are magnificently restored, others cling to survival with pumps baling out water to keep them afloat. All are treasures of the waterways.

A visit to this museum is the real deal, with opportunities that go beyond cooing and pointing from a distance. The temptation to touch is satisfied, and boats without barriers let museumgoers climb aboard to revel in the honour. The museum buildings are a maze to explore, with the old stables, the pump house, the blacksmith's forge, and the story of the canals is brought to life on information boards that accompany everything from displays of quilts to steam engines.

Porter's Row is an authentic terraced row of houses that stands as if the clocks stopped in a different era in each house. A moment is captured from the 1830s, 1900s, 1930s and 1950s as each house is kitted out with historic domestic paraphernalia and artefacts. Visitors can pop in and out of each house and unleash the inexplicable pleasure of domestic nosiness on a tour that reveals a fascinating and oddly nostalgic display of social history.

The National Waterways Museum offers an entertaining day out, but this is also a museum of tremendous national importance as it is home to the largest collection of inland waterways-related material anywhere in Britain. The vast National Waterways Archive preserves everything from the drawings and canal plans by Thomas Telford the great canal engineer, to old photographs and documents that tell the real story of the canals. This unassuming corner of Cheshire has become the custodian of a vital treasure trove of Britain's waterways heritage.

WHERE

Shropshire Union Canal
Ellesmere Port. OS SJ405771
The National Waterways Museum is a maze with as much to explore outside as inside, including its large important collection of historic boats and Heritage Boatyard. The Heritage Boatyard is the result of a partnership where volunteers work to preserve this historic boat collection and teach traditional skills to young people.
Open daily. Café and gift shop. Admission charge. Wheelchair access to most areas.

MORE INFO

The National Waterways Archive was moved to the National Waterways Museum in 2012. The Archive can be visited by appointment and can also be searched online.

www.virtualwaterways.co.uk

The waterways enthusiasts who formed the Boat Museum Society were responsible for the founding of the National Waterways Museum (then called the Boat Museum) to protect historic boats and a traditional way of life.

www.boatmuseumsociety.org.uk

T:0151 3555017 www.nwm.org.uk

Visit our website for more about the 100 Treasures, and tell us your favourite treasure www.coolcanals.com/100treasures

In landlubbing circles, the terms 'kitchen sink business' and 'cottage industry' are commonly used to describe small business ventures, but the canals have their own ideas. The 'narrowboat business' is the small business where 'small' can describe both the working business and its actual premises. Canal folk are easy liberal thinkers and their anything-goes culture is often the inspiration behind quirky entrepreneurism. Ordinary narrowboats transform into floating teashops, fudge shops, ice-cream parlours, bars, craft workshops, B&Bs...

Away from the commercial freight carried on some of the big canals, there is a growing wave of small enterprises spreading across the narrow canals of Britain in the footsteps of the old number 1s (owner-operated working boats of the canal heyday). You can go cheese tasting at the 'Cheese Boat', have your hair cut at the 'Floating Salon', tuck into a snack from the 'Cookie Boat', enjoy a good read on the 'Book Barge', indulge in a real Devon cream tea on a floating tea room, and even buy your led lighting from 'Baddie the Pirate'. Then there's candle makers, rag rug makers, blacksmiths, fender merchants, the 'Jam Boat' with gingham-topped jars for sale, and even a tiny publishing company called 'coolcanals'!

The internet revolution has brought everyone from writers to online shopkeepers. Old-fashioned values and dongles rub comfortably together as canals attract more and more visitors every year, all boosting confidence for new small floating businesses.

Food is a big success story for small businesses afloat. The trend of slow food is one thing, but on the canals it's slow eating too (4 miles an hour top speed!). There are floating restaurants in the heart of Birmingham, Stratford, London and rural places in between and beyond. The gastro experience stirs tranquil views with the gentle movement of water, and when diners grip on to their drinks as other diners arrive or leave, the ambience is complete.

The small business on a narrowboat is often a service to the vital tourist industry which helps keep our canals alive. Day-trippers can buy something special to take home from the plethora of boats that sell canal souvenirs painted with traditional roses and castles. Holidaymakers can stay in cosy floating B&Bs or book into a family-run hotel boat. And people who live aboard narrowboats rely on the coal boat that stalwartly cruises the canals to deliver throughout the winter.

Narrowboats are 7ft wide, and anything from 20-70ft long. Not much in reality, but what they lack in physical space they make up for in charm.

WHERE
On canals throughout Britain
The canals are open all day every day - just find your local canal. Trading boats can also be seen at waterways festivals and events throughout the year.

MORE INFO
Full listings of trading boats on Britain's canals can be found in our online directory.

www.coolcanals.com

Visit our website for more about the 100 Treasures, and tell us your favourite treasure www.coolcanals.com/100treasures

RIGHT: A line of trading boats at a waterways event

Sixteen locks pound together, creating a lock flight that showcases a bellowing chorus of outstretched black and white wings in celestial gesture. The Caen Hill Lock Flight does everything it can to show off. People flock here by bike, on foot, by car and in coachloads, and then there are boats too. Everyone wants to know what it feels like to stand at the bottom, or the top, of this engineering brute.

It's a bold straight climb that takes the boater more determination to climb than the towpath traveller. There's no mooring along the flight, so once a boater has started, he must finish - whereas the towpath tourist is free to linger and marvel every step of the way, and chirp at brave boats that magnificently scramble up and down the hill.

ABOVE: At the foot of Caen Hill

The route is part of the Sustrans cycle networks so bike wheels weave through ruck-sacked walkers and families of strollers. Lycra and lollipops, anoraks and cameras, walking sticks and sun cream, everyone mingles in the climb up Caen Hill Flight, but no one ever breaks into a sweat. The rise is steep and rigid yet remarkably slow with distractions that tug for attention at each step.

This is rural England, with birdsong and leafiness to prove it. Herons muse with local fish, and nature puffs throughout the climb. Meanwhile the manmade lock arms perform like an old black and white movie mistress, garlanding her way down the stairs demanding everyone's eyes.

The performance of the Kennet & Avon Canal hasn't always been so glorious. The canal was once left to decay and dry up after it was retired from the service of the Industrial Revolution. In 1962, the Kennet & Avon Canal Trust was formed and, together with British Waterways (now the Canal & River Trust) and others, a long battle began to restore the canal. The restoration project was a triumph that crescendoed in 1990 when Her Majesty The Queen navigated through lock 43 at the top of the flight to declare the canal open for boats again. The lock is now in her name, and such regal connections seem fitting for Rennie's elegant engineering masterpiece.

WHERE

Kennet & Avon Canal
Devizes. OS ST988615
Walk up the flight and then relax with a cup of tea in the teashop overlooking the locks and the open countryside beyond. Sustrans National Cycle Network Route 4 follows the towpath up past the flight - the route uses the Kennet & Avon towpath all the way from Bath through to Reading.

MORE INFO

The Caen Hill flight of 16 locks forms part of a longer stretch of 29 locks, spread over 2¼ miles leading from Seend Cleeve up to Devizes. The entire flight is a Scheduled Ancient Monument, and has been awarded a Transport Trust Red Wheel Plaque.

www.transporttrust.com   www.transportheritage.com

At Devizes Wharf, there's a small canal museum run by the Kennet & Avon Canal Trust giving an insight into the Kennet & Avon Canal from inception to restoration. Gift shop. Open daily. Small admission charge.
www.katrust.co.uk

Devizes Tourist Information Centre www.visitwiltshire.co.uk

Visit our website for more about the 100 Treasures, and tell us your favourite treasure www.coolcanals.com/100treasures

Hidden history weaves a rich tale all across the canals of Britain. And, although the biggest and best engineering marvels rarely fail to amaze, many unspectacular bridges and bends quietly conceal a historic gem of different magnitude.

In a time before the engine, horses tugged heavy narrowboats laden with cargo all across the water roads to every corner of the land. Their service to the nation was immeasurable, and still arguably under-commemorated. Deep gouge marks remain in the brickwork and ironwork of the canals today in living remembrance of the daily strain of ropes that tugged narrowboats through locks, bridges, tunnels, aqueducts and tight bends in the water road over 200 years ago.

An unwitting passerby might not notice these treasures, but the seeker can touch history with the most intimate reality. Time is bridged by rubbing your fingers through rope-sized gouges that ripple with the dry sweat of horse power.

These small grooves survive as a humbling tribute to the big characters of the cut, the gentlest giants whose forgotten names call from these hidden marks. One of the wonders of the canals.

ABOVE: One of the beautiful modern-day working horses pulling the barge, Tivertonian, on the Grand Western Canal

WHERE
On canals throughout Britain
The canals are open all day every day - just find your local canal and hunt under bridges, around locks and on sharp bends.

MORE INFO
There are only four horseboat companies still operating in the UK - at Godalming in Surrey, Hungerford in Berkshire, Llangollen in Wales and Tiverton in Devon. They all offer horse-drawn boat trips during the summer season.

www.horseboat.org.uk   www.kennet-horse-boat.co.uk   www.horsedrawnboats.co.uk   www.tivertoncanal.co.uk

The Horseboating Society works to promote horseboating and preserve its heritage and skills. www.horseboating.org.uk

Visit our website for more about the 100 Treasures, and tell us your favourite treasure www.coolcanals.com/100treasures

RIGHT: Rope marks gouged under a bridge on the Bridgwater & Taunton Canal

35 TOOLEY'S BOATYARD
A collision of two worlds

Tooley's Boatyard is the oldest dry dock in Britain. It has been in continuous use since 1790 and its daily business resiliently carried on regardless of the changes in the environment that surrounds the yard. Tooley's Boatyard is famous for many reasons, but not insignificantly because it survived in a bubble that refused to change, even when a grand new shopping centre was sprayed over the site of the historic yard.

Progress was the word that drove a nation to build a network of canals over 200 years ago, and progress in turn also cast canals aside. When Banbury wanted its new 'Castle Quay' shopping centre, Tooley's Boatyard sitting beside the Oxford Canal was controversially entangled in the plans. The boatyard that once built and repaired wooden horse-drawn narrowboats, and went on to serve the canals continuously for over 200 years has become an attraction to visit within the centre of Banbury's shopping development. Two worlds exist in one place, and Tooley's Boatyard is accessible to visitors from the shopping centre by an entrance akin to a Potteresque leap at Platform 9¾.

Tooley's Boatyard is a Scheduled Ancient Monument and its business is run by a private company, with the dry dock still providing a service to the boating community. There is also a museum and heritage centre on the site effectively merging history and the living canals in an incongruous, yet ironically ideal, spot within the happy landlubbing shoppers' world. The dock and the blacksmith's shop are listed buildings from the original 1790s site, and the dockyard buildings were more recently built, during the development of the shopping centre, to house the chandlery and art gallery.

Supporters of Britain's canals know the transport trends and economic struggles of past times have often threatened the sustainability of navigable routes across the nation. Tooley's Boatyard is famous for its connection with Tom Rolt who founded the Inland Waterways Association (IWA) during the 1940s 'war' to help keep canals open. Rolt's narrowboat 'Cressy' was docked here before it set off on its legendary voyage around the canal networks. Rolt's book 'Narrow Boat' recorded Cressy's journey and the publication had an impact that passionately and powerfully helped give a voice to the canals in an era of decline.

This boatyard melts living history into a place where the mucky-ragged everyday chores of boat life carry on, and the charisma of a no-fuss business is treasured for all that it is, and once was.

LOCATION
Oxford Canal
Banbury. OS SP457407
Open daily all year. FREE admission. Gift shop & chandlery. Guided tours around the forge, dry dock and workshops.

MORE INFO
Boat trips
The Boatyard runs scheduled boat trips. You can also hire the boat with a private skipper or to self drive.

Tooley's Boatyard is a Scheduled Ancient Monument.
They run courses ranging from basic rope handling to advanced blacksmithing.

T:01295 272917 www.tooleysboatyard.co.uk

Visit our website for more about the 100 Treasures, and tell us your favourite treasure www.coolcanals.com/100treasures

Tooley's Boatyard

Gift Shop & Chandlery

TOOLEY'S BOATYARD
THE CREATIVE HEART OF BANBURY

OPENING TIMES
TUESDAY – SUNDAY 11AM – 4PM

PLEASE NOTE, FOR DELIVERIES AND
DOCK WORK OPENING TIME IS 9AM
OR PLEASE CALL +44(0)7799054066

WWW.FACEBOOK.COM/GREASE.CCLUB

WWW.FACEBOOK.COM/CORPUSGALLERY

WWW.FACEBOOK.COM/TOOLEYSBOATYARD

WWW.FACEBOOK.COM/ASTROMOUNT

WWW.FACEBOOK.COM/DAVIDJOYBLACKSMITH

WWW.FACEBOOK.COM/SCULPTURE.LESSONS

HTTP://TWITTER.COM/#!/ASTROMOUNT

HTTP://TWITTER.COM/#!/CORPUSGALLERY

WWW.TOOLEYSBOATYARD.COM +44(0)1295 272917

My favourite treasures - chosen and written by Nigel Crowe:
Head of Heritage for the Canal & River Trust

" **Hovels, huts and lobbies are amongst the most characterful yet easily overlooked minor historic buildings of the waterways.**

Canal companies built them in large numbers for lockkeepers, lengthsmen, bridge-keepers and so on. They tended to be of brick or stone although later examples built in the years of railway ownership are of timber or even precast concrete. They all had one thing in common; small size. Hovels are often no bigger than a potting shed and typically had one doorway, a tiny window or ventilation opening and a fireplace with an external chimney.

A hovel was a permanent 'workman's hut' where canal bank staff could keep the tools of their trade, shelter from the weather and cook breakfast. Toll clerks occupied similar small buildings although these tended to be grander and located at canal junctions and busy wharves.

ABOVE: Hovel along Audlem Locks on the Shropshire Union Canal

Hovels are difficult to date; the rubblestone-walled examples on the River Avon, like that at Swineford Lock, may belong to the 1720s like the locks themselves and if so this makes them rare survivors. Most hovels range in date from the early 19th century, like the curious 'beehives' on the Shropshire Union Canal, to the late 19th or even early 20th century, like the rare barrel-vaulted example at Napton Reservoir on the Grand Union Canal. This was repaired in the late 1990s and still serves a useful purpose today. "
NIGEL CROWE

WHERE
On canals throughout Britain
The canals are open all day every day - just find your local canal.

MORE INFO
One of the modern uses of a canalside hovel is the mini vegetable, pork & poultry shop on the lockside at Audlem on the Shropshire Union Canal. The vegetable patch spreads along the lockside inviting customers to come and buy.

www.georges-pork-poultry.co.uk

Visit our website for more about the 100 Treasures, and tell us your favourite treasure www.coolcanals.com/100treasures

RIGHT: A lockside hovel on the Oxford Canal by lock 10 of the Napton Flight

The tranquil world of inland waterways doesn't need the hysterical beacons of lighthouses - except when a canal connects to the sea. The little lighthouse that sits at the entrance to the Crinan Canal is a symbol of the menacing water that lies beyond the safety of this manmade cut.

The Crinan Canal was built between 1794 and 1809 with the work of James Watt, John Rennie and Thomas Telford. It links Ardrishaig to Crinan, providing a safe, short water route that avoids the savage seas around the Mull of Kintyre. Before the canal was built, Scotland's jagged west coast had a vicious history, and even the Vikings preferred to drag their ships over land rather than face the wild route around the Mull of Kintyre.

Now the Crinan Canal is described as 'the world's most beautiful shortcut', and who wouldn't travel miles out of their way to see it? The whole canal is a Scheduled Ancient Monument, with its 15 locks and 9 miles of pure pleasure. Everyone who visits is treated to a sublime experience of Scottish proportions; and walkers, cyclists and boaters fly together in the breathtaking scenery.

ABOVE: 'Basuto' is one of the last remaining Clyde Puffers and is listed on the National Register of Historic Vessels. It can be seen in the historic boat collection at the National Waterways Museum

On this canal, Clyde Puffers have a special place in the hearts of boat spotters. They were little vessels designed to fit the Forth & Clyde and Crinan Canals, delivering coal to the west coast and carrying whisky and other produce back to Glasgow. There are only a few Puffers that have survived and two of them, 'Auld Reekie' and 'Vic 32', can sometimes be seen at Crinan Basin.

Crinan teeters on the wildest edge of Scotland, with white yachts, historic cottages, and a lighthouse that completes an idyllic picture. The unassuming lighthouse was built in 1851, only reaches 6 metres high and is unsung in comparison to the real champions that famously battle with highest dramas of the North Sea and the Atlantic.

There is no public access to the inside, which has been used as a store room in recent years, but the site is open and a white or green light (depending on direction) dutifully flashes every three seconds. An external iron ladder climbs to a vantage point and, from the ground, the hexagonal tower with its red-painted band makes the perfect scene. In the best summer weather it's tricky to visit without tripping over artists' easels or camera tripods hankering for the best angles, and, whatever the weather, the structure stands with attitude.

WHERE
Crinan Canal
Crinan. OS NR788944

MORE INFO
The entire Crinan Canal is listed as a Scheduled Ancient Monument with Historic Scotland.

The area around the end of the canal is a great vantage point for views out over Loch Crinan. 2-3,000 boats a year use the Crinan Canal so there's plenty of interest for the gongoozler. Opportunities to get on the water include chartering a yacht or going kayaking or canoeing. The entire 9-mile length of the canal also forms part of the Sustrans National Cycle Network Route 78.

Beavers have been released in the area around the Crinan Canal as part of a scheme to reintroduce the beaver to Scotland, and the Moine Mhor ('great moss') Natural Nature Reserve, one of Europe's rarest wildlife habitats, can be seen alongside the canal near Bellanoch.

Visit Scottish Canals for more info about the canal. www.scottishcanals.co.uk

Visit our website for more about the 100 Treasures, and tell us your favourite treasure www.coolcanals.com/100treasures

38 ROSES & CASTLES
Traditional canal art

Throughout the history of the world, ordinary people, who don't claim to be artists, have felt compelled to create art. Labelled as 'folk art', such work carries a burden in academic interpretation that says it is a simple form of art that is no more than an act of unsophisticated creativity. All art is a communication and the raw art of the 'common person' can reflect complex and often unintelligible messages to outsiders from a different culture. Traditional canal art has decorated 2,000 miles of waterway for over 200 years, and yet there is still no accountable theory to say why roses and castles were the recurring theme of canal art. Folk art connects us to the real lives of people who lived and worked on the canals; it is the colourful voice of traditional boat families and must be preserved for future generations to keep traditional skills and canal heritage alive.

Nobody is sure why boat families who lived and worked on narrowboats in the industrial era of the first Canal Mania painted roses and castles on the surfaces of their boats. The mystery behind the origins of these designs probably adds to their charm. Boat people were mostly illiterate, and the literate world saw little reason to write about the lives (and art) of hauliers of their era. So roses and castles remain undocumented, and theorists have been left to grapple with why the theme was so important to working boat people.

The decoration was so important to boat crews that its use could be almost obsessive. Every corner and crevice and available surface inside their boatman's cabin would have been decorated - as well as the pots, pans, and poles. Even the nosebag and harness of the boat horse didn't escape the beautiful decoration.

Perhaps it was the hardships and cramped living quarters that made boat families love such overt decorations of escapism. Was a rose the hope of a garden, and a castle the dream of a home?

One theory suggests that boat families were influenced by the designs that decorated the popular japanned metalware and papier-mache products that were made in the Midlands and transported by canal boat in the late 1700s and early 1800s. China painting in the Potteries also used a similar decoration and would have been carried by canal boats. Whatever the origins, it's clear a boatman took pride in the appearance of his boat, and saw fine decoration as a measure of rank.

Roses and castles are much more than decoration. These crudely daubed shapes in gaudy red, blue, yellow and green colours hold the richest story of Britain's canals - the story of the ordinary people.

WHERE
Adorning boats and canalia on canals throughout Britain
The canals are open all day every day - find your local canal to discover boats traditionally decorated with roses and castles, or even floating gift shops selling painted giftware. Also for sale at waterways festivals and most canalside hubs.

MORE INFO
The Waterways Craft Guild was set up to maintain the traditional skills of waterways arts and crafts. They list members (who are accredited from Apprentice up to Craftmaster) - painters of narrowboats, roses & castles, giftware and also other associated crafts, and they run courses in traditional crafts. www.waterwayscraftguild.org.uk

The Guild of Waterway Artists was founded in the 1980s to promote the best in waterways art. Their website lists members of the Guild and exhibitions of their art around the country. www.waterwayartists.org.uk

Visit our website for more about the 100 Treasures, and tell us your favourite treasure www.coolcanals.com/100treasures

RIGHT: Traditionally decorated panel inside the historic boat Ferret at the National Waterways Museum in Ellesmere Port

39 GLOUCESTER DOCKS
An army of waterside warehouses

The Romans were wise enough to pick Gloucester as a garrison to guard the River Severn, and as the river grew to become an important trade route, Elizabeth I granted Gloucester port status in 1580. But the River Severn played vicious games with vessels that struggled inland, with unpredictable sands and volatile tide levels. The Gloucester & Sharpness Canal was built to bypass the most difficult section. When the canal opened in 1827, it was the widest, deepest canal in Britain - and it must have messed with the minds of ordinary villagers who witnessed tall ships walking miraculously inland on their way to Gloucester Docks.

Trade was at its peak with the arrival of the canal and the newly built docks at Gloucester were handling exports and imports from around the world, with grain and timber as the bulk. Huge warehouses were built to store cargo; some have survived and are protected in their full glory today. Standing like towering brick boxes, the warehouses exude servile and protective expressions as they dutifully cocoon the water. Softly regimented patterns of bricks and mathematical rows of windows give the docks a strangely comforting appeal from minimalist architecture that is uniformly beautiful.

History clings in dockside ropes and rusty mooring rings, in preserved rail tracks and a steam crane, and everywhere you look there's a clue to the past. Mounted on the wall of North Warehouse there is a bell that looks quite ordinary at first glance. The bell is from the famous ship Atlas that sailed the seas to India and China for the East India Company. When the ship was dismantled in 1832, the bell found a new home in the docks. It is the bell that rang to call the start and end of every working day in the docks, and the daily sounds of bustle that once boomed from these historic docks are held in its ring.

Boatmen from around the globe once arrived in the docks, and communication was often difficult with so many different languages. Dock workers were low-paid, hard-living folk, and fighting and drunkenness was rife. Both the boatmen and the dock workers often fell into the water after drinking too much in the tavern. Amongst the human chaos, the Mariners' Church was built to care for the spiritual welfare of dock workers, seamen and folk from the canal boats. Boat people wore distinctive dress and there was an impenetrable social barrier between them and ordinary citizens, so the Mariners' Church was designed to welcome anyone even in their work clothes. It must have been a place of deep calm for a mariner living in storm-ridden climes. The church is still open today with the same balm for those who enter.

Llantony Warehouse has become the home of Gloucester Waterways Museum. The museum tells the story of the canals and invites visitors to discover amazing local sagas through exhibits that range from climb-aboard boats to displays of precious historic artefacts and hands-on activities. This canal museum is imaginative and refreshingly visitor friendly, and a must-see treasure in its own right.

The docks are paved in history on the sweat of their past, but modern sounds today click with tourist cameras and smells of mouth-watering gastro food waft across the water between the scuffle of ropes as boats moor for the night. Old life and new life are the inseparable attraction of Gloucester's historic docks.

ABOVE: Gloucester Docks with its towering warehouses and moored narrowboats

WHERE
Gloucester & Sharpness Canal
Gloucester. OS SO827183

MORE INFO
Find out all about the heritage of Britain's waterways and Gloucester Docks in the Gloucester Waterways Museum. The museum is in a Grade I-listed former warehouse with exhibits on wildlife, boating, touch-screen and interactive displays, and floating boats to explore. Open daily. Admission charge. Café next door to the museum. Gift shop. Wheelchair access (except to floating exhibits).

T:01452 318200 www.gloucesterwaterwaysmuseum.org.uk

Tall Ships Festival
Brings a taste of maritime history back to Gloucester Docks. Tall ships, family entertainment, shopping and food. Held mid August in the heart of the Docks.

www.thecityofgloucester.co.uk/tallships

Visit our website for more about the 100 Treasures, and tell us your favourite treasure www.coolcanals.com/100treasures

Scattered across the canal networks, usually perched at the waterside, there are tiny buildings that once had a huge role in the life of the canals in their working heyday. The business of the canal companies that owned the canals was to make a profit, and the toll house was where fees were collected from passing boats. Many toll houses have worn the years well as they sit in quiet glory often with new purpose as craft shops, mini museums, store rooms and even cosy homes for a lucky few.

The collection of tolls was the daily bread for the canal companies, and the toll house was a busy (if perhaps dreaded) stop for canal boats laden with cargo. Fees were charged by what was being carried and how far it was carried. Distances were measured by mileposts placed along the water routes and the weight of a boat's cargo was estimated by the markings on the boat's hull - they showed the boat's draught when empty and when full with various cargoes.

By the 19th century, a clever new system had been devised using a gauging stick. The toll collector placed the gauging stick along the side of the laden boat, and measured how many dry inches the boat had above the water line. He took four measurements to calculate an average and then used a gauge table that worked out the payment due. The clerk would then record the weight and distance travelled, along with the payment (canal museums exhibit preserved toll records), before the boats carried on.

Although each canal had its own style of architecture, toll houses were often octagonal in shape with a central door and windows positioned to see approaching traffic. They are historic buildings that have preserved their own unique charm, and enhance the built environment wherever they appear along today's canals.

WHERE
On canals throughout Britain
The canals are open all day every day - just find your local canal. Toll houses are often found at junctions between canals.

MORE INFO
Toll records are kept in the National Waterways Archive at the National Waterways Museum at Ellesmere Port, and examples can be seen at other waterways museums such as Gloucester and Stoke Bruerne.

www.nwm.org.uk www.gloucesterwaterwaysmuseum.org.uk www.stokebruernecanalmuseum.org.uk

Visit our website for more about the 100 Treasures, and tell us your favourite treasure www.coolcanals.com/100treasures

---

RIGHT: Grade II-listed toll house at Bratch Locks on the Staffordshire & Worcestershire Canal
ABOVE: The 'Stop House' (also Grade II-listed) at Braunston on the Grand Union Canal

41 TRENT LOCK
Where waters meet

Trent Lock sits on the borders of three counties, Leicestershire, Nottinghamshire and Derbyshire, and at the crossroads where the waterways history of three rivers and four canals collide with pride.

Like a ballerina in a boiler suit, the landscape at Trent Lock skips with delicate wild flora and idyllic narrowboats under the solid gaze of the shockingly beautiful chimneys of the Ratcliffe Power Station.

People flock here at weekends just to stare and unwind in the palpable presence of power. The giant energy-making chimneys do their bit, yet everything seems to sparkle at Trent Lock. It's where waters meet, and boaters battle with the breeze. The River Soar runs straight into the Trent to be gobbled by the current of the bigger river. Opposite the mouth of the Soar, the spectacular Trent Lock (built by John Varley in 1779) lets the Erewash Canal tumble into the river.

The River Trent runs about 100 miles from the Midlands to the ports of the northeast coast of England, and the North Sea beyond. Its beefy route has been used by Vikings and Romans, and there's even evidence that it was used as trade route from as early as the Bronze Age. So it wasn't surprising that the great canal engineers bagged it for their purposes too. In 1783, an Act of Parliament allowed a towpath to be constructed so that barges without sails could be towed inland. Later river locks and weirs made the journey even easier.

The Erewash Canal was one of Britain's most prosperous canals as it carried trade from local collieries, ironworks and brickworks. As well as connecting with the rivers Trent and Soar, the Erewash Canal was once joined by the busy Cromford Canal, the Derby Canal and the Nutbrook Canal. Manmade and natural waterways worked harmoniously as important transport links until the Erewash Valley Railway arrived in 1847. The new steam train stole the canal's trade and the decline began. The Erewash Canal put up a fight for survival and, through the help of a partnership of many including local people and the Canal & River Trust, is open for anyone to enjoy today.

The hub at Trent Lock is kept busy with its dry dock, pubs, tearoom and the lock itself. But history has a knack of polishing itself in the heart of the living environment. The old Canal Manager's house stands next to the lock, still watching over with a proud eye. His house is now a fabulous tearoom with evocative canalia and a gallery of fame (with signed pictures of celebrities who have visited for a pot of tea here).

The warehouse next door was once used as a toll office and a lower level was used for livestock and possibly for stabling the horses that towed boats. Even the pubs that welcome visitors to Trent Lock today are riddled with history. The Erewash Navigation Inn was built by the canal company in 1791 and it wasn't just a pub; it multi-tasked as a farmhouse too. It was known as the 'Fisherman's Rest' in the 1950s before it became the Steamboat Inn.

Despite its proximity to urban Long Eaton, the whole area is a wildlife haven with walking and cycling routes galore. In these parts there's the opportunity of catching a rare sight of creatures such as otters and water voles, and birds such as the kingfisher, goldcrest and long-tailed tit.

Life carries on at Trent Lock with the business of today, and leisure and pleasure blankets its harsher past. It is a rare place where the flash of blue from a kingfisher can dart in one moment to share the limelight with a historic built environment.

ABOVE: Ratcliffe Power Station dominates yet enhances the landscape at Trent Lock

WHERE
Erewash Canal / Rivers Trent & Soar
Trent Lock. OS SK490311
Trent Lock is where the Erewash Canal meets the river Trent and the river Soar. There are no barriers or admission charges - you can visit at any time (unless you want to visit the tearoom or one of the pubs of course!).

MORE INFO
Trent Lock not only sits where three waterways meet, but is also on the borders of three counties - Leicestershire, Nottinghamshire and Derbyshire.

The Erewash Canal's towpath is part of the Sustrans National Cycle Network Route 67 and is an easy route to cycle and walk. The Trent Valley Way, a long-distance path, follows the river Trent from Long Eaton to West Stockwith in Yorkshire.

Steamboat Inn and Lock House Tea Room are right next to the lock, and the Trent Lock pub overlooks the river Trent.

www.long-eaton.com   www.vintageinn.co.uk/thetrentlocksawley

Visit our website for more about the 100 Treasures, and tell us your favourite treasure www.coolcanals.com/100treasures

42 | DUDLEY TUNNELS
Secret underground world

Not all 'hidden treasures' are literally hidden, some just jump on the bandwagon of tourist attraction semantics. But Dudley Tunnels don't need to spin words to pull rank; they are truly hidden gems, saving their delights for the hunter.

Dudley town may be spectacularly ordinary on the surface, yet a wild experience awaits the geologist, historian and intrepid tourist who ventures underground.

While Dudley's streets go about their daily business, 250ft underground the secret world of Dudley Tunnels is a dark beastly place tangled with unworldly beauty. This underground phenomenon began during the Industrial Revolution when a staggering maze of canal miles moled their way under the Black Country.

The story really began over 420 million years ago, during the Silurian age, when limestone and coal seams formed layers beneath the ground of the West Midlands. This geology was to become prize fodder for the Industrial Revolution and, inevitably, the insatiable hunger of mass production of the manufacturing industries gobbled underground to grab precious fuel.

Navvies who had to build the tunnels risked a perilous task. Against biting draughts, they knuckled in darkness with just candles and prayers. 'Health and Safety' regulations were unheard of, and the miracles navvies performed were all part of their day's work. The 'Dudley Tunnel' was begun in 1775. It took 9 million bricks to line the tunnel and, almost unbelievably, each brick was handmade by women and children. A labyrinth of caverns and branches connect with the main tunnel, and are separated on 3 levels, by only 10 precarious feet of rock and history. As navvies pioneered with picks into the Silurian cocktail, they discovered layers of limestone and sand had become keepers of fossils. Navvies called these strangely shaped fossils the 'Dudley Bug' and craftily sold their findings to anyone interested, in a bid to boost their meagre wages (the fossil still features on Dudley's coat of arms today).

The 'Dudley Tunnel' linked Lord Dudley's limestone mines with the Birmingham Canal Navigations (BCN). Coal, limestone and iron ore were mined and then transported by canal boat to the industrial heartland of the Midlands. By 1840 the underground route carried 41,000 boats a year. With no towpath, boat crews legged and poled through tight tunnels and with the success of the transport route came congestion, leading to the construction of a parallel route, the Netherton Tunnel, in 1875.

The main tunnels had exhausted their commercial purpose in 1964, and after 10 years of little or no traffic, British Waterways (now the Canal & River Trust) decided they must abandon the tunnels. Canals usually have a knack of stirring deep passions from local people, and in reaction to the closure plans the Dudley Canal Trust was formed in 1970.

Dudley Canal Trust and hoards of helping hands all worked tirelessly to protect and promote the local heritage that visitors can enjoy today. Boat trips run regularly into the tunnels, but nobody should be fooled that this is just a boat trip. It's a journey of colours, stalactites and stalagmites, a place to see patterns lurching from a rock face playing with the subconscious in hallucinogenic games. Every so often, the darkness explodes into blinding light as the trip boat glides into parts of an old limestone quarry where the roof has fallen in to become lagoon.

Dark Cavern is too dangerous to visit now, but in 1830 a gathering of 15,000 people met here for the

lecture on geology by Sir Roderick Murchian. The Singing Cavern now hosts concerts, weddings, Christmas pantos. Over 85,000 visitors travel into this terrific grotto every year. Its popularity reflects the rapture of acoustics and art that rip the imagination.

When a trip boat pierces the darkness with its lights, passengers might spare a thought for the navvy and his fierce determination that brought prosperity to Lord Dudley. Dudley is a town that has risen and fallen on the muscles of the Black Country. Once it triumphed through the Industrial Revolution, and now it clings onto the new materialism of shopping mall culture - but the shrieks of old ghosts sailing under the ground probably yearn to yell from the rooftops that Dudley has global importance again.

WHERE
Dudley Canals
Dudley. OS SO948917
Open daily. Charge for boat trips. Gift shop. Special events and venue hire (including the unusual wedding venue in the Singing Cavern!)

MORE INFO
Boat Trips
There are hourly boat trips into the tunnels. A 45-min trip takes you on a tour of the network of tunnels - the Singing Cavern with its music and lights, miners (not real of course!) at work in Hurst Cavern, and a whirlwind of information about how man tamed the limestone beneath the earth. The boat masters are waterways oracles, willingly answering any questions about the tunnels. A full 2-hr trip through the Dudley Tunnels can be booked once a month (not Nov-Jan).

Dudley Tunnels have been awarded a Transport Trust Red Wheel Plaque.

www.transporttrust.com   www.transportheritage.com

T:01384 236275 www.dudleycanaltrust.org.uk   www.dudleytunnel.co.uk

Visit our website for more about the 100 Treasures, and tell us your favourite treasure www.coolcanals.com/100treasures

43 CAMDEN LOCK
City cool

When canals first arrived on Britain's landscape, they brought national economic boom by industry that sometimes turned peaceful moorlands into satanic millscapes, and hamlets into bustling hubs. Now Britain is gasping under the stress of its urban rash and canals have set out to help again, as they give cities vital green corridors to create tranquil spaces where they are needed most. But Camden has a will of its own: it's where the city likes being the city, and shakes its canal with urban flags, and loves its madding crowds who bump together in shoulder-to-shoulder zingy clutter.

The story of Camden began long before the canal was built. It was once an agricultural landscape with a coaching route storming through, on its way to elsewhere. In 1791 Earl Camden developed the land around the High Street and then, in the early 1800s, the canal and its twin locks arrived. The canal connected the Midlands to London Docks and to the open world across the seas. Warehouses were built along the canal and a 'roving' bridge to allow working horses to cross the canal.

After the railways took over, the trade of canals declined and Camden had to wait until the hippy 1970s before it was to be appreciated again. In 1971 a market moved into an unwanted building and something exciting was about to happen. Camden became a tourist hotspot, with the world flocking to its now famous markets. With an 'anything goes' culture, the outdoor markets spread with unbridled street fashion, joss sticks, ripe mangoes and rainbow hats. This is a city canal where life does its own thing, and the next generation of 'young people' follow with their own twist. But whatever the trends of fashion dictate, at Camden Lock it seems tie-dye will never tire and watching all the action pass by from waterside bars will never stop being cool.

WHERE
Regent's Canal
London. OS TQ266840

MORE INFO
Although known as Camden Lock, there is no lock by that name - Camden Lock is the area around the twin Hampstead Road locks in the heart of Camden. Twin locks are an unusual feature on the canals, and were created on busy canal routes to allow boats travelling both up and down the canal to use the locks at the same time.

Hampstead Road Lock and the roving bridge across the twin locks are separately Grade II-listed.

Boat Trips
Take one of the regular trips on a traditional narrowboat between Camden and Little Venice (passing through Regent's Park and London Zoo).

www.jasons.co.uk www.londonwaterbus.com

Visit our website for more about the 100 Treasures, and tell us your favourite treasure www.coolcanals.com/100treasures

RIGHT: The twin Hampstead Lock at Camden, with the roving bridge beyond

44 WATER
Mighty canals from little raindrops grow

"A man's best things are nearest him,
Lie close about his feet."
Richard Monckton Milnes (1809-1885)

Human nature often leads us to take for granted those things we most care about, especially when they are dependably there. Without water there are no waterways. A narrowboat without water is ludicrous, and a duck without water is the saddest sight. Holiday boats would grind to a halt, swans would fly away, fishermen would go home and walkers wouldn't linger. Canals depend on the sky; frankly, rain is the real treasure of the entire canal networks. Without nature, Britain's manmade canals would be useless.

Canals need rain, but they can't rely on rainfall alone. The Canal & River Trust is responsible for looking after the canals of England and Wales and has to manage water supplies to maintain healthy working canals.

There are more boats using the canals now than during the era of Canal Mania at the time of the Industrial Revolution over 200 years ago - and water shortage is a constant problem to overcome, especially during seasons of drought. Every time a boat passes through a broad lock it uses around 50,000 gallons of water, and a narrow lock uses 30,000 gallons.

Supplies of water for canals are stored in reservoirs, and water levels are carefully monitored on the same day each week in order to see any changes - and respond by feeding thirsty canals from the most suitable reservoir. Management of water levels can also be helped by the use of pumps. Some canals use pumps to move water from a bottom lock back up to a top lock to save water.

Since canals first arrived on Britain's map they have miraculously linked regions by marvels of engineering. Yet, regardless of entrepreneurial power, and engineering genius, without water the canals would never have been more than mere desperate ditches, tragic containers of redundant lock gates and dead pumping stations. Water has always been the living spirit, the power and the point of the entire canal system. And, not insignificantly, every living creature that shares the waterways environment with us, helps create the unique world of canals that is a joy to visit.

WHERE
On canals throughout Britain
The canals are open all day every day - just find your local canal.

MORE INFO
The water for the majority of the canal system in England and Wales is managed by the Canal & River Trust, while the water for Scotland's canals is looked after by Scottish Canals. The entire system uses the equivalent of two billion bathtubs of water.

www.canalandrivertrust.org.uk www.scottishcanals.co.uk

Visit our website for more about the 100 Treasures, and tell us your favourite treasure www.coolcanals.com/100treasures

RIGHT: A winter's morning in Stourport Basins

45 BRADFORD ON AVON ROUTE
Busy hub for boats, bikes and boots

To the outside onlooker, the canal at Bradford on Avon breaks the expected norm. Everyone on the canals usually wants to watch boats on the water, but this is a place where boats do the watching as swarms of bikes revel in the freedom of the perfect towpath ride.

Families of bikes are propped in piles in the doorways of quaint cafés along the waterside. People come in lycra and knobbly-kneed shorts, with panniers of picnics and lashings of ginger beer. The towpath is part of Route 4 of Sustrans National Cycle Network, and its popularity is fed by its proximity to Bath and Bristol.

There are tandems, trailer buggies, tricycles and bicycles for hire on every corner of Bradford on Avon. There are canoes for hire and dayboat trips too, but the towpath is determined to rule this section of the Kennet & Avon Canal; cyclists can pedal all day without meeting a car, whether they cycle the entire route or simply potter around the canalside hub in Bradford on Avon.

Bradford on Avon was once a busy weaving centre, and some of the old buildings remain, but the 14th-century Tithe Barn dominates the canalside landscape. The Great Tithe Barn watched the canal being built and now sits by its side as tourists flit and coo with spinning cameras.

The canal carries the breeze of nearby Bath with its Royal Crescents, Jane Austen, Roman soldiers, Palladian mansions and Regency houses. Bradford on Avon has stone terraced buildings and is sometimes described as a miniature Bath; but that misrepresents the quirkiness of this Wiltshire gem. The canal is a heady mix of Georgian charm, two-wheeled madness and enough cafés and bars to fill the bottomless pit of the hungriest free-wheeling child. Dick and Jane's café bar overlooks the water, and its gingham facade flirts with a deliberately dangerous menu that asks its customers to survive its famous belly-bursting Boatman's Breakfast. But of course, it's not only boaters who can take on the challenge!

Speeding cyclists don't belong anywhere in the slow world of the canals, but when ambling clumps of bikes chatter as they crunch their way along the towpath, they melt into the cacophony of walkers, sightseers and boaty charm of busy Bradford on Avon.

WHERE
Kennet & Avon Canal
Bradford on Avon. OS ST825602

MORE INFO
Hire bicycles, day boats or Canadian canoes from the Lock Inn Café, or if you prefer a more relaxing visit, take the trip boat from above Bradford Lock.

Take a look inside the medieval Tithe Barn then visit the surrounding artists' studios, galleries, shops and tearooms.

www.tithebarnartscrafts.co.uk

Bradford on Avon Tourist Information www.bradfordonavon.co.uk

Visit our website for more about the 100 Treasures, and tell us your favourite treasure www.coolcanals.com/100treasures

RIGHT: Bikes piled up outside a canalside pub

LONDON CANAL MUSEUM
The ice well in the heart of the city

The trick up the sleeve of London Canal Museum is that the building which houses the museum is as fascinating as the collections inside.

The building is a former ice house built in 1862-3 for the business of the famous ice-cream maker, Carlo Gatti. Long before refrigeration had been invented, Britain needed ice to keep its food fresh and chill its drinks, and for medical purposes. To the relentlessly resourceful Victorian, the obvious solution was to import shipfuls of nature's own ice from Norway. Ice arrived on large ships and was then carried by canal boat into London.

Carlo Gatti's building has been preserved with two vast ice wells under its floor where Norwegian ice was once stored. Visitors to the museum can stand and stare down into the ice well; invariably transfixed by the magnitude of the outrageously overblown operation that went on behind the scenes of a simple ice-cream for the 'Downton Abbey' brigades of a bygone era.

The museum looks over Battlebridge Basin (built 1823) where modern day narrowboats are moored. They go about their daily lives, with their own mini fridges usually whirring merrily in their galleys, and no homage is paid to the trials of Gatti's ice wells. Past and present mingle in this museum, and its setting is its asset. Leave King's Cross or St Pancras International Station, slip down a side street and you'll find this gem hidden just a stone's throw away from the big city. Inside this historic building, old London tells its intriguing story.

This is a London museum, built gloriously in London coloured bricks, with a focus on London's powerful waterways heritage, and displayed within the context of canals across the country. London Canal Museum is a real treasure tucked cosily away right in the city, and open for the world to visit.

ABOVE: London Canal Museum on the canalside in Battlebridge Basin

ABOVE: Historic photograph of men sawing ice from a frozen lake

LOCATION
Regent's Canal
London. OS TQ304833
Open Tues to Sun & Bank Holidays (closed other Mondays). Small admission charge. Gift shop. Wheelchair access. Short-term mooring just outside the museum should you arrive by boat!

MORE INFO
The museum's collection includes tools of the ice trade, artefacts of the canal and its people, horses, and boats. You're invited to climb aboard the narrowboat Coronis to experience the daily living conditions of a boat family. There are also lace plates, Measham teapots, canal art, boat trips, screen displays, and a fascinating collection of oral history 'Precious Memories Preserved'.

The entire museum can be privately hired as a truly unique event venue.

T:0207 7130836 www.canalmuseum.org.uk

Visit our website for more about the 100 Treasures, and tell us your favourite treasure www.coolcanals.com/100treasures

My favourite treasures - chosen and written by Nigel Crowe:
Head of Heritage for the Canal & River Trust

> **Signs and notices are found all over the waterways. Many are smart black and white ones; others are survivors from the past and bear historic names and messages.**

They were put up by canal or railway companies at bridges, boundaries, reservoirs and so on. They draw attention to weight restrictions, hazards or private property.

The earliest canal signs were made of wood and had painted lettering. None of these survive outside museums. Later signs are rectangular, square or lozenge-shaped cast iron plates either mounted on a post or attached to a building or structure. They typically bear a company name and more or less straightforward instructions in raised lettering. The lettering was often painted white on a black background. Later, British Waterways (now the Canal & River Trust) added its famous blue and gold paintwork, some of which still lingers in odd places.

The largest signs were loading plates which were put up by the Great Western Railway. They had detachable sections so that numbers could be varied. There are good examples of these lozenge-shaped signs on canals like the Kennet & Avon and the South Stratford and several of the waterway museums have similar examples displayed.

NIGEL CROWE

ABOVE: These days signs aren't only authoritative, they're interactive, informative and educational and part of the life of the canals (this sign is on the Droitwich Canal)

WHERE
On canals throughout Britain
The canals are open all day every day - just find your local canal.

MORE INFO
There are examples of early canal signs in the National Waterways Museum at Ellesmere Port, and other waterways museums such as Gloucester, London and Stoke Bruerne.

www.nwm.org.uk www.gloucesterwaterwaysmuseum.org.uk www.stokebruernecanalmuseum.org.uk

Visit our website for more about the 100 Treasures, and tell us your favourite treasure www.coolcanals.com/100treasures

RIGHT: Lozenge-shaped sign on the
Monmouthshire & Brecon Canal near Pencelli

THE CHOCOLATE CANAL
Narrowboats bulging with temptation

My favourite treasure - chosen by Julia Bradbury:
TV Presenter, Ramblers Vice-President and walking personality.
"My favourite 'treasure' of Britain's canals would have to be the 'chocolate'
canal of course! When I was walking the Worcester & Birmingham Canal for
the 'Canal Walks' BBC TV series and book, I walked past Cadbury's chocolate
factory at Bournville – what chocoholic could resist...!?!"

While the Napoleonic Wars were raging on the continent, Britain was also busy tucking into its new discovery - chocolate. In the 1800s, a clean-living Quaker family, with the now-famous name Cadbury, tempted a nation to the perfect sin. The Worcester & Birmingham Canal brought the cocoa bean to the factory that eventually made the chocolate bar; and the Cadbury's factory at Bournville keeps its doors open today - sweet-toothed visitors enter at their own peril.

The story of chocolate began with ancient Mayan and Aztec civilizations who sucked drinks from the cocoa bean long before European explorers had even set sail to 'discover' the Americas. When Columbus stumbled upon the bean, he didn't rate its chances of popularity, and it wasn't until the early 1500s, when the conquistador Hernan Cortes brought the bean back to Europe for kings and queens to chomp, that its potential was realised.

ABOVE: Julia Bradbury on the Worcester & Birmingham Canal during filming of the BBC's 'Canal Walks' series

By the 1800s the new luxury chocolate drink was all the rage, served in the coffee houses emerging on almost every street corner of London. In 1824 John Cadbury opened a grocery shop in Birmingham selling drinking chocoate and cocoa; and by 1831, brothers John and Benjamin Cadbury had started manufacturing chocolate as a brand.

The canals were behind the success of Cadbury's chocolate boom. Cocoa beans arrived on seagoing vessels from afar, and were transhipped to smaller canal boats to make their way inland along the Gloucester & Sharpness Canal to Frampton on Severn where milk was added and the process of turning the cocoa beans into chocolate crumb began. Cadbury's recipe continued its journey by narrowboat to their factory on the Worcester & Birmingham Canal where it was made into chocolate.

Mr Cadbury's chocolate bar was soon ready to seduce generations of taste buds all across the globe, but the philanthropic Quaker family business had to be founded on ethical trade. Cadbury boycotted cocoa beans from African plantations where slavery was rife, and he insisted that profit in business didn't need to compromise social responsibility at home. The Industrial Revolution was bringing furious economic growth in Britain, often at the disregard of the poorest workers in the worst factories and mills of the manufacturing industries. In 1893 John Cadbury's son George built a village, called Bournville, for his workers. His aim was to provide

ABOVE: Today's café culture, where the Worcester & Birmingham Canal reaches the heart of Birmingham

quality housing, with open spaces for the wellbeing of the community. Workers in the Cadbury factory could enjoy a good standard of life, with the overriding acceptance that drunkenness was not acceptable in a clean-living village - and, to Mr C's word, there has never been a pub built in Bournville.

The chocolate canal follows its course from Worcester to Birmingham, with an irresistible journey between two cities, rambling through rolling countryside that carries the tastiest history every step of the way. Only the strong-willed traveller can escape the attraction of a visit to Cadbury's World.

WHERE
Worcester & Birmingham Canal
Bournville. OS SP050811
Cadbury World is open daily February to November. December / January limited opening times. Admission charge.
Cadbury café and gift shop - the world's biggest Cadbury Shop. Wheelchair access. Children's play area.

MORE INFO
Explore the fascinating village of Bournville around Cadbury World. George Cadbury wanted to create a healthy environment that his workers could afford and stipulated that at least one-tenth of the estate should be 'laid out and used as parks, recreation grounds and open space'.

George Cadbury set up the Bournville Village Trust in 1900 to care for and maintain the growing community - this work carries on today and has now expanded well beyond Bournville itself.

www.bvt.org.uk

T:0844 8807667 www.cadburyworld.co.uk www.cadbury.co.uk

Visit our website for more about the 100 Treasures, and tell us your favourite treasure www.coolcanals.com/100treasures

Burnley is an earnest reminder of the rewards and sacrifices Lancashire holds in its history that was bound to swing with the pendulum of the textile industry. The 'ordinary' town of Burnley was once the weaving capital of the world, but now the industry has gone, leaving only a handful of textile manufacturers in the area. The Weavers' Triangle is a modern name that was given to a triangular area alongside the Leeds & Liverpool Canal and, in a triumph of living heritage, it has become one of the best preserved 19th-century industrial districts in Britain.

Historic buildings wrap around the canal in the centre of town - weaving sheds, spinning mills, engine houses, warehouses, foundries and houses. On their own, these buildings tell a tremendously important story of social and economic history, and the visitor centre at Burnley Wharf helps with extra information.

Any text book can say how a loom works, but words can't capture the satisfaction of standing in the presence of a real loom that towers and owns its space with the pulsating clickty-clackt of the weave in action. Any modern day visitor who finds a quiet moment in the streets of the Weavers' Triangle, and ponders over the thought of those sounds of Victorian times in the area, must gasp at the fact that by the second half of the 19th century Burnley had a staggering 79,000 looms.

Textiles have been made in Burnley since at least the Middle Ages and cottage industries grew throughout different eras until Burnley became an industrial town in the 18th century. The invention of the Spinning Jenny and the steam engine, and the arrival of the Leeds & Liverpool Canal connecting trade routes to the world, changed the fortunes of the textile industry and led to the boom in population growth of Burnley. Industry needed workers and as they were recruited from other areas, back to back houses and tenements were provided as homes crammed between warehouses and factories. The Weavers' Triangle has preserved some of these dwellings to show to horrible truth of overcrowding that the workforce endured.

Conditions at work were equally shameful, as employees worked long hours over unguarded machinery with health risks that would frighten today's safety obsessed culture. An emotional fever challenged the status quo during the early 19th century as hand loom workers went on strike for the right to earn a minimum wage. There were riots and hard times before a final brutal fall in 1861 left the whole industry in turmoil. The Civil War in America had cut off supplies of cotton and Lancashire's mills were in trouble. Soup kitchens opened to offer soup, clothes, clogs and solace to unemployed mill workers.

When the Suez Canal opened in 1869 a new short cut opened up a new source of cotton from India. The political and economic benefits kept the Weavers' Triangle in business until war threatened. World War I slaughtered Burnley's workforce, cut off its raw materials and its markets. The decline was inevitable, and made more hopeless by World War II. The struggles of the North that followed left its population branded and labelled as different from the South. Lancashire's labours once helped Britain's purse to bulge and, today, treasures such as the Weavers' Triangle are being protected as an investment for future generations to be proud of.

The Weavers' Triangle is a built environment stacked with human stories, local characters and skills that make bricks and mortar bulge with heart felt heritage. The Weavers' Triangle holds the cultural values the industrial north once stood for, and showcases the importance of preserving national heritage.

ABOVE: Historic photograph of fly & 'Jay' at the Manchester Road Warehouse in Burnley on the Leeds & Liverpool Canal 1890 (National Waterways Archive)

WHERE

Leeds & Liverpool Canal
Burnley. OS SD838322
See an original mill engine working in Oak Mount Mill (the mill started life as a spinning mill in the 1830s, and its chimney is the tallest still standing in Burnley), and have a go at weaving in the Visitor Centre. There are also guided towpath walks, and visits to the Burnley Embankment, one of the engineering wonders of the waterways. FREE admission. Visitor Centre, café, gift shop. Limited wheelchair access.

MORE INFO

Several of the warehouses and other buildings in Burnley are Grade II-listed.

The Weavers' Triangle Trust is working to preserve Burnley's textile heritage & one of the finest surviving Victorian industrial landscapes in the country.

T:01282 452403 www.weaverstriangle.co.uk

Visit our website for more about the 100 Treasures, and tell us your favourite treasure www.coolcanals.com/100treasures

WORLD WAR II PILLBOX
Home front on the water

My favourite treasures - chosen and written by Nigel Crowe:
Head of Heritage for the Canal & River Trust

"As soon as World War II began, the British people turned to 'digging trenches and trying on gas masks' as Prime Minister Neville Chamberlain put it.

General 'Tiny' Ironside was given the job of turning Britain into a fortress, with a defended coastal crust and a series of inland stop lines to delay invading German forces. A number of these followed the courses of various canals. One of them was the Oxford and Grand Union Canals Stop Line that was intended to defend the industrial Midlands. It is still scattered with the remains of wartime structures, including anti-tank blocks, hairpins, hedgehogs (moveable lines of bent or upright steel rails) and pillboxes built of concrete that was often reinforced with old bed springs.

Pillboxes were designed to protect gunners and 28,000 of them were built across Britain in the opening years of the war; by the summer of 1940 one was being built every 20 minutes. Their sites were surveyed by the Royal Engineers and they were built by local contractors, often in great haste – one of the Stent prefabricated pillboxes at Napton on the Oxford Canal has several back-to-front concrete panels. These pillboxes might look flimsy, but their concrete walls are over half a metre thick. They were manned by the Home Guard, who could have faced an advancing German army had things turned out differently. Seventy odd years on, these humble remains from the worst war in history have become part of our national heritage.

A good 'defended' section of the Oxford and Grand Union Canal Stop Line runs between Bridges 113 and 116 at Napton in Warwickshire. This section has octagonal anti-tank obstacles rolled into fields, mounting points for steel rails on the bridges and square concrete pillboxes teetering on the edge of the canal. **"**
NIGEL CROWE

WHERE
Scattered on canals throughout Britain

MORE INFO
Pillboxes were constructed across Britain because of the real threat of a German invasion during World War II. The Pillbox Study Group's website maps the UK's pillboxes, of which over 6,000 survive, including those along the canals.

www.pillbox-study-group.org.uk

Visit our website for more about the 100 Treasures, and tell us your favourite treasure www.coolcanals.com/100treasures

RIGHT: A pillbox hiding on the canalside near lock 13 on the Oxford Canal at Napton

51 CHANDLERY
Shopping, the canal way

It's the high street shop of the secret waterways world. You won't find a chandlery in any shopping mall across the land, but step down into the world of canals and the chandlery will be there on the waterside; a beacon for boaters and the curiosity shop of towpath tourists. This isn't just ordinary shopping, this is the Aladdin's Cave of boaty paraphernalia and canalia.

Essentially the chandlery is a hardware store for the boater, it's the place to buy anything from a brass cleat to a new anchor; but for the window shopper, it's also a den of bits and bobs and unintelligible gadgets, and something 'that might come in useful one day'. People come to fondle brass bolts and fancy tiller pins, rummage through sailors' clothing and stroke giant rolls of mariner's rope. And there's everything for a house, except in miniature: narrowboat-sized fridges, sinks, cookers, portholes, floating key rings, galley pots and pans, and that perfect door mat.

In the early canal years, before canal tourism, boat families who lived aboard working boats got their maintenance supplies from boatyards and rustic stores along their routes. It was the renaissance of canals with the development of leisure boating that created the business opportunity for the modern chandlery. Midland Chandlers, one of the most recognised names, has been operating for around 30 years, and now has four well-stocked stores. Limekiln Chandlers is another well-known name, a family-run shop started in 2002 by David and Carol Elwell. "You can get everything from a postcard to a portaloo from us" they say; and Sam, their daughter paints traditional canalware for their shop in Stourport's historic basins.

As well as the specialist chandleries, most holiday hireboat companies have a small chandlery attached to their boat centres. And there are always less known names running no-fuss chandleries from working boatyards, and raggy sheds, all across the canal networks. A narrowboater in overalls can reliably find a pot of K99 water resistant grease for his stern gland here, but perhaps the browsing towpath tourists might not fit in so well.

So the chandlery has many guises: it's a purpose-built building with well-designed lines of crisply lit shelves, or it's a deranged den of organised clumps - and now, in the throngs of the internet shopping revolution, it has also become the elusively accessible, and differently browsable www store too.

WHERE
On canals throughout Britain
The canals are open all day every day - just find your local canal.

MORE INFO
Full listings of all canalside chandleries in Britain can be found in our online directory.

www.coolcanals.com

Visit our website for more about the 100 Treasures, and tell us your favourite treasure www.coolcanals.com/100treasures

RIGHT: Limekiln Chandlers in Stourport is housed in a historic former warehouse in the basin

Tardebigge sits at the heart of Worcestershire's countryside, in a staggering landscape that rattles with 30 locks designed to carry boats in a rise of almost 220ft in just over 2 miles. The Tardebigge Flight is the longest lock flight in Britain.

The Worcester & Birmingham Canal is a narrow canal with an extraordinary number of locks all along its route, and the Tardebigge Flight is its glorious nemesis.

The canal's original purpose was to connect from the River Severn to carry coal, grain, tea, sugar, cocoa beans, timber and other general goods. It was a busy canal and crews of those old working boats faced a torturous journey on a canal plagued with locks and tunnels. The Tardebigge Flight must have been a miserable challenge, to be tackled with guts and precision if delivery times were to be met.

Crews on the Worcester & Birmingham Canal often used pairs of donkeys and mules rather than horses to tow their boats. These unfortunate creatures were cajoled through the Tardebigge by desperate crews with time against them. The lock gates were partially opened while the weight of the water was still 2ft below the level necessary to open the gate easily. The crews would wedge a block of wood between the gates to create an extra paddle in an act of insane haste. Post-Victorian society would call this a breach of 'Health and Safety' rules, dubious animal welfare, vandalism of our canals, and all eyebrows would raise at the devil who would dare.

Today's towpath tourists join in the cheery camaraderie that pervades on one of the most popular cruising rings for holiday boats. Climbing the Tardebigge Flight is an experience that bonds and cheers travellers on the water and on the towpath. Tardebigge Top Lock is one of the deepest in Britain, with a rise of 11ft. Originally there was a boat lift planned on the site, but it was replaced by a gaspingly deep lock in order to save money and the technical problems associated with the lift.

The Tardebigge Flight was the bulldog that refused to let any hill get in its way, now it is a rural delight, set in an uplifting panorama.

WHERE
Worcester & Birmingham Canal
Tardebigge. OS SO993692
The Tardebigge Lock Flight spreads over two miles, and is surrounded by open countryside.

MORE INFO
If you climb up the banks of the reservoir part of the way down the flight, you can see the Malvern Hills in the distance.

Tardebigge Top Lock is Grade II-listed. Just beyond the lock is a plaque commemorating a meeting which took place here in 1945 between Tom Rolt and Robert Aickman which led to the founding of the Inland Waterways Association.

There's a display at Tardebigge Wharf of the hull of a former steam tug 'Birmingham', which started in 1877 to tow boats through the Tardebigge, Shortwood and Wast Hills Tunnels on the Worcester & Birmingham (up to then, boats had to be legged through the tunnels, with the donkeys which towed them having to walk over the top).

Visit our website for more about the 100 Treasures, and tell us your favourite treasure www.coolcanals.com/100treasures

RIGHT: View over the Tardebigge Flight from the reservoir

IDLE WOMEN BADGE
Wartime work on the waterways

In the throngs of World War II, Britain cried out to its own people to help the war effort. The 'boys' were told to take up arms in battle, while the 'girls' kept the home fires burning. And, in the absence of the male workforce, old stereotypes of gender roles had to shunt into new territory. Jobs traditionally done by men in peacetime had to be done by women. Farmers' fields were worked by the 'Land Girls' and, in a similar fashion but in smaller numbers, the canals had a new band of hard-working women. They wore a badge with the initials IW, to show that they were working for the war effort on the Inland Waterways. The vital work they did is now honoured by the incongruous nickname Idle Women that came from those initials.

The true story of the 'Idle Women' of the canals is an extraordinary account of a group of wartime volunteers who worked tirelessly for the benefit of the nation. It all began with an advertisement placed by the Department for War Transport in the national press in the early 1940s. It asked for volunteers to work on the waterways and although no boating experience was necessary, it insisted that only women 'of robust constitution' need apply. All the successful applicants duly found themselves operating boats which carried up to 50 tons of essential supplies along the nation's waterways. After only six weeks' initial training they

might be transporting important parts for the Spitfire aeroplane from London Docks to Birmingham, or collecting coal from the Midlands to take to London. A round trip could take three weeks, after which the women had the option of a week's unpaid leave. Their task was anything but idle.

The volunteers were mostly young women from middle class backgrounds with no experience of manual labour, and the traditional boat families that were born and bred on the waterways were initially wary of the newcomers that they called Idle Women. But from the diaries of the Idle Women, it is clear that they and the traditional boat families earned mutual respect as they worked hard under each other's gaze.

Living aboard a narrowboat was a new experience for young women who had replied to a mere ad in a paper, and not all could cope with the cramped and intimate conditions. Idle Women's diary notes recorded the blunt basics of boat life 'using buckets for loos' and 'sharing a tiny back cabin with someone else.' As well as enduring personal inconveniences, the women had to load and unload the cargo, repair the boat's engine when needed, chop firewood, prepare meals and cook on black ranges. But personal accounts from many of the women show the freedom that the canals gave them was often a joy too. Olga Kevelos, one of the Idle Women, has been quoted as saying, "Life on the waterways was very hard and the days unpredictable. We worked 18 hours a day, were usually cold, wet and hungry but it was immense fun and full of the unexpected."

Daphne March, Molly Trail and Kit Gayford, Margaret Cornish, Helen Skyrme, Olga Kevelos, Emma Smith... the names are a roll of honour for some of Britain's feisty wartime women. Around 45 women, aged from 18 to mid-thirties, worked on the inland waterways of England between 1943 and 1946. They were the female few that a country owed so much to. The Idle Women's badge that was once worn unceremoniously during a busy day's work is now a symbol that honours these special women of the canals.

ABOVE: Historic photograph of Idle Women trainees
OPPOSITE: The infamous IW badge which gave the women their nickname of Idle Women (both National Waterways Archive)

WHERE

Shropshire Union Canal
Ellesmere Port. OS SJ405771
The IW badge is part of the National Waterways Archive at the National Waterways Museum in Ellesmere Port. There are also displays about the work of the Idle Women at most other waterways museums.
www.nwm.org.uk www.stokebruernecanalmuseum.org.uk www.gloucesterwaterwaysmuseum.org.uk

MORE INFO

A plaque in honour of the Idle Women and to commemorate their part in the war effort was unveiled at the Canal Museum in Stoke Bruerne in October 2008. www.stokebruernecanalmuseum.org.uk

'Idle Women' by Susan Woolfitt is one of many books detailing life as a trainee working on canal boats in World War II.

Visit our website for more about the 100 Treasures, and tell us your favourite treasure www.coolcanals.com/100treasures

*My favourite treasures - chosen and written by John Bridgeman CBE TD DL:
Vice Chairman of British Waterways and Trustee of the Canal & River Trust.*

*"Restless hearts, it has been a long time,
Out here on the journey, for a glimpse of paradise,
It's getting hard to find a place to go,
Where peaceful waters flow;"* Chris De Burgh

It is certainly hard to find anywhere so delightfully peaceful as the waters of the Montgomery Canal. It never paid a dividend to any of its original founding shareholders but it is certainly paying dividends to its visitors in the 21st century. Today it offers so much to so many: navigation and destinations for boaters, still waters for canoeists, flora and fauna for naturalists, trails for cyclists, ramblers and walkers and a wealth of welcoming country cafes, pubs and restaurants all in an ongoing restoration project driven by a remarkable band of volunteers.

The Canal originally had two main purposes - to distribute lime and other supplies to farms on and around the route and to transport goods from Newtown through Welshpool and onto the Shropshire Union Canal – a distance of some 53km. It was originally seen as a potentially important transport link between the Severn and the Mersey. It also follows the River Severn for several kilometres to the north-east of Newtown and passes through Pool Quay, a former river port at the limit of commercial transport up the River Severn from Bristol. Probably the best known Pool Quay cargo was Welsh Oak, for which the area was famous, and which was shipped down to the naval dockyards in Bristol. Even today slow-growing, tight-ringed Welsh Oak is the material of choice for the Canal & River Trust, making heritage lock gates at its Stanley Ferry Workshop in Yorkshire.

The Montgomery Canal leaves the Llangollen Canal at Lower Frankton in Shropshire. It is then navigable, with controlled access by a Canal & River Trust lockkeeper, for some 11km as far as Gronwyn Bridge. Early in the journey one passes through Graham Palmer Lock, a fitting tribute to the canal restoration pioneer and founder of the Waterway Recovery Group who died tragically young at the age of 49 and to whom inland waterway lovers owe so much. En route one can enjoy the friendly Queen's Head in the village of the same name, the Navigation at Maesbury Marsh and the not to be missed Canal Central at Maesbury Marsh just past Spiggots's Bridge, No 80.

Further along at Redwith Bridge, the restoration effort is extending the navigable waterway to a winding point at Crickheath. The next phase will be to Llanymynech. Volunteers from the Inland Waterways Association, the Friends of the Montgomery Canal, The Shropshire Union Canal Society, The Waterway Recovery Group and the Montgomery Waterway Restoration Trust have been determinedly working on restoring the Montgomery Canal to high standards of craftsmanship since 1969. Volunteers come from all over the country to work here – from Newcastle upon Tyne to Devon; some families are introducing a young third generation to the effort. The Montgomery Canal through to Newtown will one day be re-opened. There has never been any doubt.

OVERLEAF LEFT: The Montgomery Canal, bursting wth wild flowers and grasses
OVERLEAF RIGHT: Frankton Locks on the Montgomery Canal

At Llanymynech, in Shropshire, the canal crosses the border into Wales although signage in Welsh extends for many miles into the English stretch. At the border is the marvellous Llanymynech Heritage Area. Here one can see old wharves and an early Hoffman Kiln for lime production, a process which made possible semi-continuous output of lime coupled with a massive improvement in energy efficiency. It's a technology still used in ring furnaces today to bake electrodes for a number of modern industries.

It is around Llanymynech where one realises what riches the Montgomery Canal provides for naturalists: Meadowsweet, Marsh Woundwort and Yellow Water Iris, with Damselflies (including the white-legged Damselfly) and Dragonflies, shoaling Bream and Roach, and Coots, Mallards, Moorhens, Swans and Wrens in abundance. The Montgomery Canal is a declared Site of Special Scientific Interest (SSSI) for over two thirds of its length and a Special Area of Conservation in Wales; it is also one of the most important sites for Floating Water Plantain and for Grass-wrack Pondweed in the world.

The Montgomery Canal is one of the most canoe-friendly waterways in Britain (there are five one-day routes described on the Canal & River Trust website). Canoes and kayaks are not allowed in locks for good safety reasons and so canoe trolleys are a great asset on the Montgomery Canal.

On the English side, much has been done to rescue the canal from the reckless abandonment in the 1960s but there is still much to be done in Wales. The full economic potential of a restored waterway will not be available to the people of Powys until local government makes good the dislocation of the canal at major road crossings. Economic analyses of the benefits attributable to restoring Scotland's Lowlands Canals and England's Kennet & Avon Canal show that benefits exceeded costs by a factor of more than three to one. All of Powys will benefit from bringing the Montgomery Canal back to life.

The Montgomery Canal descends from the Welsh Border to the River Severn with bottom pound at Red Bridge (No. 106) and surplus water draining down into the river. The stretch from Pool Quay to Welshpool is named the Prince of Wales Length and His Royal Highness has four times visited the Montgomery Canal to witness progress with its restoration. The Prince of Wales Committee in association with the Variety Club of Great Britain made a substantial contribution to restoration of the Pool Quay flight. His Royal Highness later became Patron of The Waterways Trust and in 2012 he became Patron of the Canal & River Trust.

Eventually we will all be able enjoy the navigation from Frankton Junction down to Pool Quay and the River Severn. Once more there will be a navigable waterway from the Mersey to the Severn passing through the stunning countryside of the Welsh Marches… Where peaceful waters flow… **"**
JOHN BRIDGEMAN

WHERE
Montgomery Canal
Lower Frankton. OS SJ370318

MORE INFO
Walkers will already be familiar with the Montgomery Canal - the Severn Way follows the Montgomery Canal towpath all the way from Newtown to Welshpool and the Offa's Dyke Path, one of the National Trails, joins the towpath for a while above Welshpool. www.severnway.co.uk www.nationaltrail.co.uk

Narrowboats can cruise the short navigable stretch from Welsh Frankton, but canoeing is possible along much of the canal's length. A licence to use canals is included free as part of the membership package for both the British Canoe Union and Canoe Wales. www.canalrivertrust.org.uk www.canoewales.com www.bcu.org.uk

Llanymynech Heritage area www.llanymynech.org.uk

Visit our website for more about the 100 Treasures, and tell us your favourite treasure www.coolcanals.com/100treasures

55 LITTLE VENICE
London's big secret

The Changing of the Guard, Madame Tussauds, Oxford Street, Fleet Street, the Ritz and the glitz of the city makes London one of the most visited places on earth. But while London is busy blasting its horns and blowing its trumpets, the Regent's Canal is a quiet oasis hidden in a parallel world that remains stubbornly unspoilt by speed and the furrows of the rabid race.

The Regent's Canal quietly trots through London by the backdoor, and Little Venice is the 'pool' of water where the Regent's Canal meets the Grand Union Canal. The towpath curves with the pool and gives London its laziest tea break with a view. There's even a converted barge to make sure the refreshments are right on hand.

It's said that the poet Robert Browning, who used to live in a house overlooking the Regent's Canal, gave Little Venice its name as he compared his London view with Venice. In turn, the small island in the middle of the 'pool' is called Browning Island after him.

A stroll along the canal passes moored narrowboats with that city live-aboard look, and stucco-clad Regency housing creates the mood of this patch. The canal was named after the Prince Regent, later to become George IV, and the architectural calm order gives this urban canal perfect grace. But this is wild London too, with the canal cutting through London Zoo. Captive creatures can watch through their netting and squawk at moorhens, grebes, coots, geese and other wildfowl which roam free, and lanky-legged herons can often be seen sunbathing by the canal.

Every May Bank Holiday, Little Venice goes mad, with hoards turning up for the famous Canal Cavalcade. Boats cram side by side, stalls line the waterside, and that special waterside festival feeling grips the crowds. But for most of the year, Little Venice is the city's secret oasis, where the rush hour is a distant concept, and water and boats slow the pace... and nature does its own thing.

WHERE
Regent's Canal
London. OS TQ262818
Where the Regent's Canal joins the Grand Union Canal.

MORE INFO
Little Venice is the perfect spot in the city for a waterside coffee. Or take a walk from Little Venice along the towpath to Camden through Regent's Park and London Zoo.

The Canalway Cavalcade is held at the beginning of May each year, and this normally calm and tranquil oasis becomes a hive of boats, bunting and partygoers!

The Cavalcade is organised by the Inland Waterways Association www.waterways.org.uk

Boat Trips
Take one of the regular trips on a traditional narrowboat between Camden and Little Venice (passing through Regent's Park and London Zoo).

www.jasons.co.uk   www.londonwaterbus.com

Visit our website for more about the 100 Treasures, and tell us your favourite treasure www.coolcanals.com/100treasures

RIGHT: Little Venice is an oasis of calm in the city

56 21ST-CENTURY NARROWBOAT
The iconic image of the canals

When summer sunshine pelts down over Britain, the word 'canal' draws in a deep, dreamy-eyed breath, followed by one exhaled Pavlovian mantra 'narrowboats!' It's the romantic vision that pops all blisters of stress and soothes the psyche of a nation in an instant.

When James Brindley was asked to build the first canals in Britain, his brief was to build a transport route to speed up the Industrial Revolution - and even in the most fertile corners of his imagination, he probably couldn't have foreseen the transformation, in over 2 centuries, from his haulage routes into leisure havens.

The evolution of the narrowboat is a contradiction, with changes that could have made modern boats sit unrecognisably next to their ancestors, yet the canals have a knack of maintaining their accolade of being unspoilt by progress. The skinny, overworked 'starvationer' boats that laboured inside the Duke of Bridgewater's mines influenced James Brindley when he built his narrow locks and canals. The idea was to save as much water as possible by keeping his canal locks narrow. The narrow lock dictated the maximum size of a canal boat at 72ft long by 7ft wide, and since canals haven't changed in over 200 years, that remains the shape of a modern narrowboat.

ABOVE: A shared moment at the lock

The 'starvationer' was a mine labourer, blackened by the filth of coal dust, with ribs that protruded from its bony carcass. The modern narrowboat hasn't grown any wider, but it is fat with decadent comforts and brass polish. Microwaves, showers, Jacuzzis and sofas, and anything money can buy is designed to niftily cram into a luxury floating 'Tardis' these days. Even cleaning can be a hobby for today's boater. Mere housework in land life becomes a community activity on a canal boat. Conversations between boaters invariably involve accounts of drying out the bilges, touching up paintwork, refilling the grease gun and checking the weed hatch. The mop lives like an ornament on the roof of the boat, and is often decorated in narrowboat stripes (and is itself cleaned after it has swilled the decks). Passersby watch and stop to chat over the chores in hand. The camaraderie around boat-life is a treasure of the canals in its own right.

And it's not just boaters who love boats. Walkers and families on bikes crane necks to catch every moment of a passing boat. Water travel is fascinating to the gongoozler whose sole purpose is to revel in the passive pleasure of watching boats mess about on the water. No one would bring a deckchair to sit by the side of a modern motorway or lean over a road bridge to watch cars manoeuvre into the parking slots of a car park, but on the canals the prize pastime is to lean over tight bridges waiting for the next boat to try its skills (or perhaps magnificently scratch its top coat).

Boats were traditionally made of wood, but the 21st-century narrowboat is usually a steel shell. Inside, modern warmth has spray foam insulation between the steel shell and the wood interior, and central heating if the owner wants. Cruiser or trad stern, josher bow or tug, specifications are all part of the lingo. And the

names signwritten on the outside panels of boats tell their own stories – 'Serendipity', 'Spending the kids' inheritance', 'Narrow escape'. Often two names are bonded to create oddities such as 'Daveanne', 'Joliz', 'Meander'! Everything is in a name. And if you are new to canals, it is best to warn you that the laidback canal boater can rarely be agitated, but woe betide anyone who commits the cardinal sin of mistakenly calling his narrowboat, a 'barge'.

The narrowboat is one of Britain's most iconic images, and the tranquil scene of a boat cruising along a leafy landscape is the quintessential picture of Britain's canals... and the pride and joy of canal people. The busy industrial days have gone when traditional working narrowboats scurried from port to factory with cargoes to unload and reload again. Today, the leisurely narrowboater cruises wherever the whim takes. It's the slow boat that isn't meant to hurry, nor hanker after a destination; and it's the journey that must be savoured, knowing time at the tiller is time well spent.

WHERE
On canals throughout Britain
The canals are open all day every day - just find your local canal.

MORE INFO
Full listings of all canal boatbuilders in Britain can be found in our online directory. www.coolcanals.com

57 GRAFFITI
Art in the shadows

My favourite treasure -
We would have asked the brilliantly elusive Bristol born hoody, Banksy, who has become the super-spraycan-man of the underworld, to choose his treasure of the canals - but since we couldn't find him, we will hazard a guess that he might choose graffiti!

We searched under the darkest canal bridges on dank urban nights, and hunted down the most popular aerosol streets of Britain in an attempt to find the graffiti artist extraordinaire, Banksy. No one sees him, but wherever he leaves his mark, the world wants to follow. His controversial daubings have tested a nation to accept the unacceptable - graffiti. Art form or menace? Somehow, under the cover of the night, on streets dripping with darkness, he has successfully sent the hegemonic hoohah of the fine art world into a spin. He messed with our minds when he famously took over Bristol Museum and Art Gallery in 2009, and over 300,000 people turned up to see it. He has turned heads on the Regent's Canal in London with paint-inspired satire and given the canals graffiti to treasure.

Graffiti is 'a piece of writing or drawing scribbled, scratched or sprayed on a surface'. It's hardly surprising it is not a modern invention. Graffiti was cool over 200 years ago and has historic interest on the canals:

"Dates and initials carved into brick or stone often record momentous years or events, and occasionally carved pictures may be found. One striking example of picture graffiti occurs at Awbridge road bridge on the Staffs & Worcs Canal. Here, on one of the capstones, there is a carefully carved sailing ship; a sleek vessel with tall masts and a line of gun-ports. The ship appears to represent one of the early ironclad warships which served in the Royal Navy from the 1820's onwards. If this is so, then romantic notions that it was carved by Napoleonic prisoners-of-war are unlikely to be right. Much more likely is the idea that it was cut into the stone by some bored resident of Trysull Workhouse, which once stood almost cheek-by-jowl with Awbridge road bridge and was demolished long ago. Visitors to the Staffs & Worcs Canal can see this historic graffiti..."
Nigel Crowe, Head of Heritage Canal & River Trust, 2012

Loved and loathed, graffiti has always been at home on urban canals. The swift mark of the unknown artist, the genius, the yob, the youth, the unheard voice of society has scratched the facade of Britain's canals with screams of joy, anger, humour, poverty, fear and frustration.

In its many modern forms it can be everything from public exhibitions of the finest art money can't buy, to the unholy bile of the disenfranchised, or the aerosol diarrhoea of daring dissent; or it might be simple acts of self-interest in banal daubs by those who scarcely understand why passersby should know 'I waz ere', or it can be just fabulous happy decoration that adds zazz to plain urban drabness. All graffiti is communication: it makes invisible people's voices visible - sometimes offering stark viewing of otherness, and sometimes mirroring society in its most thrilling form.

Canals have always been unique in bringing people of diverse backgrounds together in an intimate linear space. In the early days of canals it was entrepreneurs, navvies, boat families, merchants and thieves. Today it's tourists, traders and more: a traveller from anywhere can bump into another, and locals everywhere mingle with passersby.

ABOVE: A Banksy on the canalside at Camden on the Regent's Canal in London

Without people, canals are nothing; so, for good and bad, graffiti is a living, if transient, part of its society. The debate goes on whether graffiti can ever be art, and it may be contentious to have chosen graffiti as a treasured object of Britain's canals. Yet, even at graffiti's most depressing level when it seems no more than vandalism, the culprit who sets out to mindlessly deface the canal environment may inadvertently be displaying subversive recognition that canals are special. On that we all agree. So although the decent person's leisure and pleasure never wants to be jolted by hostile graffiti, graffiti can enhance the canal environment when presented in aesthetically pleasing ways. In the countryside and in cities, canals are tucked away from the chaos and mad crowds of the real world; they lead us into secret havens where we can find a space to be at peace with ourselves, and unleash the knots of the unresolved. Graffiti art, at its best, is entertainment to that end.

WHERE
On canals throughout Britain
The canals are open all day every day - just find your local canal.

MORE INFO
From a hoody-distance, the elusive maestro of canal graffiti frolics with journalists and crowds who reliably flock to see his work. www.banksy.co.uk

Visit our website for more about the 100 Treasures, and tell us your favourite treasure www.coolcanals.com/100treasures

58 STARVATIONER
Prototype for the narrowboat

A skinny little boat known as the starvationer played a remarkable role in the mid-1700s as it was destined to influence the emerging story of Britain's canals. The starvationer is believed to be the prototype for the narrowboat, and this tiny vessel helped shape the thoughts of the great canal engineer James Brindley when he first designed Britain's canal and narrow lock systems.

Francis Egerton, the Duke of Bridgewater, used starvationers in his mines at Worsley in the 1700s. The boats worked several miles underground, scurrying along a 46-mile labyrinth of manmade channels into the mine system. The starvationer was made of oak and elm to be sturdy, and had a point at both ends, which was practical for its purpose in a tight mine. Its name is attributed to its narrow bony appearance with exposed rib shapes, and the dark task of this mine boat only adds to the lament in the name.

In the mines, the starvationer would be loaded with coal and then moved through the levels on an ingenious inclined plane. The engineering audacity of the first Canal Mania was birthed in the Duke of Bridgewater's mines.

Like most grand engineering and entrepreneurial feats along the canals, it was ordinary men who laboured to bring success to fruition. In the Duke's amazing mines, men spent dark days 'walking' starvationers

through the tunnels by lying on their backs using their feet on the roof of the tunnel to move the unpowered boats. The coal was transferred to bigger boats which were then towed further along the cut. Boats as big as 70ft long by 7ft wide were built for the job, and these 'box boats' were most likely to have influenced Brindley when he came to construct the narrow locks that became the main feature all across the networks of Britain's canals.

The mines were profitable, but the Duke wanted to reach markets quicker and more economically than by clumsy tracks over land. So he asked James Brindley and John Gilbert to plan a route that could get his coal from the mine to Manchester by boat. His pioneering business logic gave Britain its first completely manmade inland waterway, the Bridgewater Canal. It was an insane idea that turned out to be a roaring success. The canal was lock free as it followed the contours of the landscape. Brindley stunned sceptics, and even when he met the River Irwell, the worst obstacle in his route, he innovatively built Barton Aqueduct to enable his canal to carry on regardless.

The starvationer was an instrument in the early movement that created a 2,000-mile network of

ABOVE: Historic photograph from the National Waterways Archive of the boats outside the Duke of Bridgewater's mines at Worsley
LEFT: The Starvationer on display in the National Waterways Museum

canals in Britain. Today the National Waterways Museum has one of these important boats as an exhibit. In its robust glory, sitting in dry silence for museum visitors to admire, it somehow seems to sum up the success of an entire canal system. But its message doesn't cling on its own self-importance, it rings with the core notion that no single boat, or bridge, or engineering marvel or entrepreneur with brave ideas could have made the canals work on their own - it was people of all skills and class that made canals work.

WHERE
Shropshire Union Canal
Ellesmere Port. OS SJ405771
One of the last remaining Starvationers, a 30ft by 3½ft wooden boat, is on display in the National Waterways Museum in Ellesmere Port. Open daily. Café and gift shop. Admission charge. Wheelchair access to most areas.

T:0151 3555017 www.nwm.org.uk

MORE INFO
The Barton Aqueduct was originally built to carry the Bridgewater Canal over the river Irwell, but was replaced in 1893 by the Barton Swing Aqueduct when the Manchester Ship Canal was built. Barton Swing Aqueduct is one of the wonders of the waterways, as it swings the canal effortlessly out of the way for the huge ships on the Manchester Ship Canal below.

www.bridgewatercanal.co.uk

Visit our website for more about the 100 Treasures, and tell us your favourite treasure www.coolcanals.com/100treasures

59 GONGOOZLER'S PERCH
Prized position for the boat spectator

The gongoozler is the object of well-meant mockery and envy along the canals, for he, or she, is the person engaged in the laziest pursuit of all - doing absolutely nothing except watch boats messing about on the water. The skill of the beautifully idle gongoozler is to stake prime spots where the most entertaining boat activity is likely to happen. Locks, bridges, aqueducts, junctions and anywhere a tricky boat manoeuvre might cause a drama are all popular perches for the serial gongoozler.

The origin of the word gongoozler isn't precisely known, but one theory suggests it might come from Lincolnshire dialect 'gawn' and 'gooze', meaning stare and gape.

It was recorded in the glossary of a book written by Henry Rodolph de Salis, titled 'Bradshaw's Canals and Navigable Rivers of England and Wales' (1904). L T Rolt also used the word in his book, 'Narrow Boat', in 1944, but the word didn't become popular until after the 1970s.

Now canal slang has officially made its mark, with its entry in the Oxford Dictionary which describes the gongoozler as a noun, 'an idle spectator'. Although dictionaries haven't pampered to canal slang, the premise must stand that if there is a noun 'gongoozler', it must be possible that there should be the verb to gongoozle, to go gongoozling or to be gongoozled.

In the working canal era of the 18th century, to be called idle would be a most foul accusation indeed; but along today's tranquil waterways the leisure seeker pursues idleness with pride. Messing about in boats is one way to enjoy Britain's canals, gongoozling is the other.

WHERE
On canals throughout Britain
The canals are open all day every day - just find your local canal.

MORE INFO
Any junction, the place where two canals meet, is bound to cause a bit of a commotion. The antics of boaters who get into a tangle with their tillers, and the bumps between bows of passing boats make prime drama on the canals for the gongoozler. But there's plenty of beautifully polished boats to watch just from the canal side at any hub of boating activity such as a marina, boatyard or flight of locks.

The best perch would be standing on a bridge in a flight of locks near a busy junction - Fradley Junction attracts summer hoards, who turn up to stand and stare at the fun as the Coventry Canal meets the Trent & Mersey Canal. An unforgiving 90-degree turn from the Coventry Canal onto the Trent & Mersey Canal cruelly catches boaters out, and the water's edge outside the pub at the junction bears the crash marks.

Visit our website for more about the 100 Treasures, and tell us your favourite treasure www.coolcanals.com/100treasures

RIGHT: The junction of the Coventry and Trent & Mersey Canals at Fradley - a perfect spot for gongoozlers

 My favourite treasures - chosen and written by Nigel Crowe:
Head of Heritage for the Canal & River Trust

❝ **Diamonds, crosses, triangles, lazy 'S's, double 'X's, stars and anchors; these are some of the masons' marks which can be discovered on stone buildings up and down the waterways.**

Marking stones was an ancient practice dating back to at least the 12th century. The men who hammered out their signatures in this way were the banker masons, who worked and shaped stone blocks on a bench before passing them on to fixer masons who performed the actual construction. The strange marks identified each stone with a particular mason. In this way mistakes could be traced and payment by measure made. Counting up the different marks on a building usually gives a rough estimate of how many masons worked upon it.

The stone faces of John Rennie's great triumphal arch, Dundas Aqueduct on the Kennet & Avon Canal, are scattered with masons' marks, the relatively soft limestone lending itself readily to chiselled impressions. Look on the south-eastern wing in particular, next time you are visiting the Bath area. ❞
NIGEL CROWE

ABOVE: A mason's mark on Dundas Aqueduct

WHERE
On canals throughout Britain

MORE INFO
The canals are open all day every day - just find your local canal.

Visit our website for more about the 100 Treasures, and tell us your favourite treasure www.coolcanals.com/100treasures

RIGHT: A mason's mark concealed, yet clearly visible, on Dundas Aqueduct, Kennet & Avon Canal

This iron beauty, a staggering monument of maths and art, is one of the wonders of the canals. The amazing Anderton Boat Lift is the world's oldest boat lift - and is miraculously still open for business today, attracting over 110,000 visitors every year by boat and on foot for the ride of their lives. It's affectionately known as the 'Cathedral of the Canals' and the visitor needs no explanation.

The boat lift was built in 1875 by Edward Leader Williams and Edwin Clark, with the purpose of lifting boats over the cliff edge between the Trent & Mersey Canal and the River Weaver 50ft below. Businessmen at the start of the 18th century were crying out for a speedier trade route as Cheshire's salt industry was set to boom in world markets. Prior to the lift, salt was hurled clumsily down wooden chutes to land on boats, known as Weaver Flats, lying in the water below and then relayed downstream.

A masterpiece of engineering was set to defy the drop and duly, with dynamic Victorian eccentricity, an Eiffel-esque structure of knitted ironwork was erected to tower over the River Weaver. Two humungous 252-ton caissons (tanks) with sealing doors perch on hydraulic rams, linked ingeniously to make the descending tank force the ram under the other tank to lift it in equal measure to the descending tank. In doing so, the steam-powered boat lift is operated on maximum economy. With a steam engine and pump, the hydraulics could lift a 72ft 60-ton narrowboat from canal to river in less than 10 minutes.

ABOVE: Narrowboat entering the Lift

The salt industry had given the world an ironwork treasure, yet ironically it was the salt industry that led to its closure, as the salt in the River Weaver polluted the hydraulics of the lift and corrosion had its way. In 1908 the structure was converted to an electric motor system that drove the two tanks. A new frame was added around the old, with the addition of a machinery deck. Each tank was counterbalanced by over 250 tons of cast-iron counterweights attached by wire ropes. Then 72 geared pulley wheels kept the lift moving.

The demon rust returned again, and in 1983 Anderton Boat Lift gave up its fight, thwarted by lack of funding. The Cathedral of the Canals mandatorily mustered support from outraged canal enthusiasts determined to keep this treasure alive. The Waterways Trust (now merged with British Waterways into the Canal & River Trust), the Heritage Lottery Fund and umpteen waterways people clubbed fresh funding for the restoration of the 2001 structure. They replaced the hydraulics to replicate the original ram system and the 1908 structure was retained as a static open air museum piece. The project whistled through the equivalent of one mile of welding and dismantled over 3,000 bits of ironwork puzzle to be cleaned and reassembled. A tangled Meccano-game of manly proportions.

Anderton Boat Lift is one of only two working boat lifts in Britain today (Falkirk in Scotland has the other). Thanks to this riot of Victorian ingenuity, visitors can turn up reliably during the travelling season on the waterways for a mad, dripping ride in a boat lift. For boaters and walkers, the rise and fall bridges their journey between the Trent & Mersey Canal and the River Weaver in spectacular style. And sightseers can turn up just for the ride. Whatever way the visitor arrives, everyone leaves the lift as if it was an ordinary day again - except their bulging faces rarely manage to conceal the stories bursting to be told.

ABOVE: The Anderton Boat Lift from the River Weaver

WHERE

Trent & Mersey Canal

Anderton, Northwich. OS SJ647753

Opening times vary. Admission FREE to Visitor centre, exhibition area, café and gift shop (car park charge). Charge for boat trips. Picnic and children's play area. Wheelchair access. Discount for Friends of the Canal & River Trust.

MORE INFO

Boat Trip

The Anderton Boat Lift is impressive enough from the ground but you can enjoy a 30-minute boat trip and get a boat's eye view from inside the lift. 'Edwin Clarke' is a glass-topped trip boat taking you 50 feet up from the River Weaver to the Trent & Mersey Canal above. The boat masters are waterways oracles, willingly answering any questions about the Lift.

The Boat Lift (and its surroundings) is a Scheduled Ancient Monument, and has been awarded a Transport Trust Red Wheel Plaque.

www.transporttrust.com   www.transportheritage.com

T:01606 786777 www.andertonboatlift.co.uk

Visit our website for more about the 100 Treasures, and tell us your favourite treasure www.coolcanals.com/100treasures

"...coolness is knowing when to slow down, take time out, commune with nature, savour pleasures too precious to be rushed..." (Daily Telegraph, 2009)

Imagine a world with no cars, no rush hour, a place where people still nod and smile at each other... somewhere that lets nature and man enjoy the rhythms of the day together.

The secret world of canals is an escape from modern noise. Water, boats, precious wildlife, charismatic landscapes basking in living heritage, and the good old-fashioned camaraderie of slow culture - these make the sounds of the canals. The clinking of mooring rings, the hoot of a moorhen, the splash of a duck, the scuttles of creatures in the hedgerow, the friendly chatter of people...

Travel defines canal life, but to stand still for a while and listen to the sounds of the water is time to cherish.

Visit our website for more about the 100 Treasures, and tell us your favourite treasure www.coolcanals.com/100treasures

63 | THE TURF
A Tudor gem

Few places on earth can feel solitary at the same time as welcoming people. There's a secret spot in Devon that attracts hoards every year for the rare thrill of that perfect moment. The Turf is a honeypot site where a canal wrestles with nature, as the land ends and the sea tries to bully its way along the Exe Estuary.

The river Exe connects the historic city of Exeter with the sea. The estuary sprawls with shifting sandbanks and a deep water channel that doesn't always behave well. The Romans and the Danes tackled the water route during their reign over the city, and navigation through the 13th century helped Exeter to prosper. But eventually over-silting and extortionate tolls made the route impassable. John Trew was set the challenge of cutting a manmade water route to run parallel with the river. The first stage of the Exeter Ship Canal was built in 1567, over two centuries ahead of the great canal era.

A canal that swells with stories from Tudor times is bound to appeal to visitors, and history clenches the imagination immaculately as tall masts sway in the salty breeze and the smell of rusty mooring chains clink from modern boats on the canal.

The canal was extended further in the late 1600s and the Double Locks (between Topsham and Exeter) were built to replace the original trio of locks. It was so unusually large that small boats were carried round the lock on rail tracks to save the water, time and effort needed to fill the chamber. The canal continued to grow as an important link with Exeter, and by the 17th century the city became one of the richest in England.

James Green completed the canal build to its full 5¾ miles in 1827. From Topsham Lock to Turf Lock there is still a towpath on either side of the canal. This was unusual in its time, and was designed to allow two horses to work together to pull heavier loads. Horse power (at 2hp) was the pride of this stretch of canal and yet, now that horsepower is manmade, the end section of the Exeter Ship Canal is hallowed as a car-free route. There's no point scratching at maps to find a road to the Turf, this is for boots, bikes and boats only.

In summer months, clusters of outdoor folk pilgrim to the Turf. There's only one way there and one way back, and the journey is part of the experience. This is not remote England (there's a car park for those who only want to walk the half mile to the end of the canal) but the explicit exclusion of road access gives the final stretch a unique vibe.

At the very end of the canal, the final sod of earth at the petering edge of land marks the point where a manmade waterway hands over to nature. The wild winds of the river estuary sweep waves at the canal and grip the voyeur. The grass sways gracefully and there's a soulful air from the triangular spot where water surrounds three sides of the land. The chance of seeing rare species of wildlife enjoying their freedom perfects the moment - avocets feed on the mud flats, geese, curlew, warblers, lapwings and hoards of unrecognisable creatures swarm in the perfect loneliness of a corner in Britain where cars aren't allowed.

The Turf is a trickster when it invites the visitor to inhale the solitude. A cherry on the icing awaits the pilgrim who reaches the end of this canal - a fantastic pub. The Turf Inn isn't like other canalside pubs; it speaks seaside lingo, with the tide times above the bar. Open fires, local ales, and dogs galore that are genuinely welcome. England at its watery best.

ABOVE: Where the aptly named Turf meets the Exe Estuary

WHERE

Exeter Ship Canal
Turf Lock. OS SX963860
The Turf is where the Exeter Ship Canal meets the Exe Estuary. There are no barriers or admission charges - you can visit at any time (unless you want to visit the pub of course!). The Exeter Ship Canal's towpath is part of the Sustrans National Cycle Network Route 2 and an easy route to cycle and walk.

MORE INFO

The Exe Estuary is a designated Site of Special Scientific Interest (SSSI), a Special Protected Area (SPA) and a wetland site of special interest (Ramsar), due to the wealth of wildlife living here.

The Turf pub is in an enviable position on the tiny spit of land between the canal and the estuary.

www.turfpub.net

www.exeter.gov.uk   www.exe-estuary.org

Visit our website for more about the 100 Treasures, and tell us your favourite treasure www.coolcanals.com/100treasures

Instinct leaves us prone to perching objects of historic importance on protective pedestals or behind barriers - but many of Britain's precious historic boats travel the waterways valiantly bearing the brunt of inevitable bumps from other passing boats.

Saturn lives on the canals of the North West and Wales. She is the last horse-drawn Shropshire Union fly-boat in the world. Under the care of The Saturn Project she cruises the waterways slowly carrying the story of speed from a hundred years ago.

Shroppie fly-boats were the floating Ferraris of their time. Other boaters would move aside, giving priority to these high speed bullets that were admired for their fine design and skilled crews bulging with success.

ABOVE: A close-up of Saturn's signwriting

Shroppie fly boatmen were regarded as elite, with dapper appeal as they worked to precision timing in four-man teams and a relay of horses around the clock. (The dawn to dusk cruising rule was only introduced later when holiday boats became popular on the waterways). The business of the Shroppie fly was to carry perishable goods and the Shropshire Union Canal Carrying Company expected its boats to race to deliver on impossible schedules. This boat is a living treasure that holds the story of speed, ironically the antithesis of today's canal culture.

Saturn was built in 1906 in the Shropshire Union Canal Carrying Company's Chester docks. She was employed to transport cheeses from Cheshire and Shropshire to markets in Manchester and around the North West, Midlands and Wales.

When railways arrived, and speed was redefined, the fly-boat service was relegated to carrying coal and chocolate products until they became redundant by the 1950s.

The boat had to find a new purpose or face the fate of decay. Peter Froud, a pioneering waterways campaigner and early Inland Waterways Association member, bought Saturn in 1955. He fitted a cabin and an engine. Then, in 1958, he gave Saturn a career change, launching her as a hotel boat business under the name of Canal Voyagers. Tourism on the canals was teetering with intent and Saturn was setting a pattern for future hotel boats to follow. A pioneer once again.

Time and seasons passed and, one by one, each Shroppie fly-boat disappeared from the water - until Saturn became the last relic of a lost era. Saturn was bought by British Waterways Wales and Border Counties and, under the partnership of the Saturn Project, the Shropshire Union Canal fly-boat Restoration Society restored the boat. It took 4 years, £87,000 and the help of many. In 2005 she was relaunched and this nugget of treasure was saved for future generations.

Visit Saturn today and you'll be greeted by volunteers loaded with passion and troves of waterways knowledge. Saturn is a precious treasure of Britain's transport heritage and those who climb aboard will sense the privilege.

ABOVE: Saturn at the Historic Boat Gathering in Audlem in Shropshire

WHERE

Saturn mainly travels the canals of the North West and Wales, and appears at festivals and events throughout the year. There is always the opportunity to climb into the tiny cabin to get a taste of how the boatmen would have lived, and volunteers are on hand to answer any questions you may have.

MORE INFO

For a full itinerary of Saturn's travels, visit the website. Saturn is looked after entirely by volunteers and they are always looking for ways to raise funds.

Saturn is listed on the National Register of Historic Vessels (NRHV), and was given the honour in 2012 of carrying the Olympic torch-bearer across Pontcysyllte Aqueduct in Wales as part of the route to London. How fitting that Saturn, once the fastest canal boat, should 'speed' at walking pace with the Olympic Torch!

www.nationalhistoricships.org.uk

Shropshire Union Fly-boat Restoration Society www.saturnflyboat.org.uk

WOODEN PATTERN
Craftmanship shaping the canal environment

My favourite treasures - chosen and written by Nigel Crowe:
Head of Heritage for the Canal & River Trust

" Wooden patterns form a slightly obscure branch of waterway heritage. They were basically templates which were used to make cast iron objects and many can still be found hidden away in lofts and workshops around the canal network. One of the best collections is housed at Ellesmere Yard on the Llangollen Canal.

Traditionally, castings were made using the sand moulding method. A wooden pattern was pressed into sand in a mould box. Molten iron was poured into the mould and, on cooling, the sand was broken away to reveal the cast iron object. For simple casting of, say, a bollard, a sand mould would be made in two halves. Although the mould was lost each time, the wooden pattern could be used repeatedly to form new ones.

Patterns were made from an even-grained wood that was free from splits and shakes and easily worked. Great skill was needed to carve bollards, mileposts, lock gate fittings, racks, pinions and the dozens of other items of ironmongery required on a working canal. Small castings were made at canal yards like Ellesmere, larger items would be sent to a local foundry.

There are good samples of patterns at the waterways museums and other examples are scattered throughout the country. Careful reuse of some of these historic patterns is possible. When the great Pontcysyllte Aqueduct in Wales was repaired a few years ago, original patterns for some of its iron components, like the handrails, were found and used to recreate entirely authentic replicas that sit happily alongside the originals. **"**

NIGEL CROWE

WHERE
On canals throughout Britain
The canals are open all day every day - just find your local canal.

MORE INFO
Examples of historic wooden patterns can be seen at Ellesmere Yard on the Shropshire Union Canal, in the National Waterways Museum at Ellesmere Port, and in other waterways museums such as Gloucester, London and Stoke Bruerne.

www.nwm.org.uk www.gloucesterwaterwaysmuseum.org.uk www.stokebruernecanalmuseum.org.uk

Visit our website for more about the 100 Treasures, and tell us your favourite treasure www.coolcanals.com/100treasures

RIGHT: Pattern Shop at the National Waterways Museum in Ellesmere Port

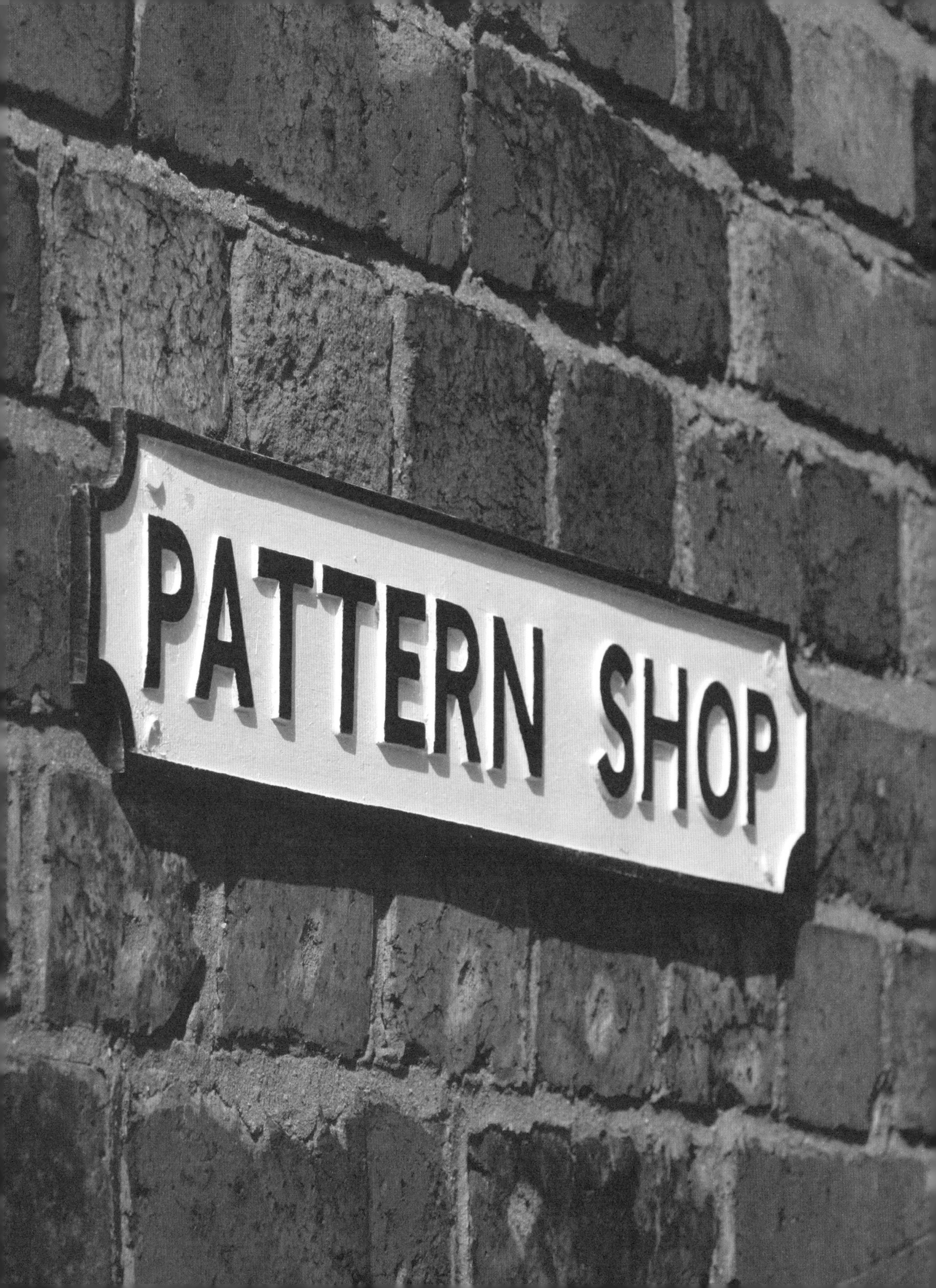
PATTERN SHOP

66 INTERNATIONAL SLAVERY MUSEUM
The only national museum of its kind in the world

The International Slavery Museum is located in Liverpool's Albert Dock, at the centre of the World Heritage Site and in the zone where ships once set off on their heinous mission to collect cargoes of people who had their freedom stripped from them. The museum says it is 'the only national museum in the world dedicated to the history of the transatlantic slave trade and its legacy'. Any museum that exhibits the unacceptable truth about the denial of human rights and the execution of gross atrocities in the pursuit of power and profit is an uncomfortable 'must' to visit. The revolting so-called trade that enslaved some people whilst building the prosperity of others was a complex web of connections in the years between 1500 and 1900, and the industries of Britain's canals were inevitably entangled.

No book that speaks about the joys of Britain's canals would be ethically complete without facing the issue of slavery. Bristol, London, and Liverpool had ports that thrived on the slave trade, and by the second half of the 18th century it is estimated that around ¾ of all European slaving ships left from Liverpool. One reason for the dominance of this Lancashire port could be that it was served well by canals and rivers. Textiles from Lancashire and Yorkshire, salt from Cheshire, pottery from Staffordshire and metal goods (horrifically including chains and guns) from the Midlands were all transported along the inland waterways to Liverpool - from where they became part of the trade triangle.

The trade triangle was a three-way journey that started in goods from Europe being shipped to Africa where they were exchanged for people. The second part of the trade triangle involved the Middle Passage which was the 6 to 8-week voyage across the Atlantic to the Americas. Africans were piled in the holds of ships that ignored all cries of humanity, and not all survived the journey. On arrival in the Americas, the African people who had successfully fought off death during the passage were sold into slavery. The third stage of the triangle then carried resources from the American plantations home to Europe, including such 18th-century riches as sugar, coffee, tobacco, rice and cotton.

The profits of the trade triangle fed the lifestyle of high society with coffee shops in London and gentlemen's coveted tobacco supplies. Many other industries were built on a pedestal of wealth rooted in the slave trade. Even unwittingly businesses could benefit from private investors and bankers made wealthy by indirect connection to lucrative trade in slavery.

There were influential philanthropic canal people who joined the Africans in their revolt against slavery. Quaker families such as Cadbury refused to buy resources from plantations based on slavery, and showed by example that business could succeed from fair trade and ethical investment. Josiah Wedgwood supported abolition and produced a medallion with the image of an enslaved man, with the inscription 'Am I not a Man and a Brother?'. Wedgwood's medallion became the ionic image of the abolitionist movement. The political push of Quakers, William Wilberforce and Olaudah Equiano (the voice of African abolitionists) added muscle to the organised rebellion of the African people and eventually in 1807 the slave trade in the British Empire was ended. In 1833, slavery itself was abolished.

When the sun shines hardest on any strawberries and cream day by the canalside, people nod and smile together as they mess about in boats or stroll the towpaths. The evils of slavery seem to belong elsewhere, but the insidious story of slavery travels even through Britain's beautiful canals. The International Slavery Museum tackles the truth with brutal sensitivity. It manages to exhibit a positive reconciliation of what has passed and what can yet be done, which has to make this museum a treasure of the canals.

ABOVE: Merseyside Maritime Museum in Albert Dock - the International Slavery Museum is on the 3rd floor

LOCATION

River Mersey
Liverpool. OS SJ340898
Open daily. FREE admission. Café, restaurant and gift shop. Wheelchair access. Picnic benches outside by the water.

MORE INFO

The Museum is on the 3rd floor of the Merseyside Maritime Museum in Albert Dock. As well as its permanent galleries, the museum runs a schedule of temporary exhibitions.

Albert Dock is one of the earliest enclosed docks in the world, and is at the heart of the Liverpool World Heritage Site.

Liverpool UNESCO World Heritage Site www.liverpoolworldheritage.com   whc.unesco.org/en/list

T:0151 4784499 www.liverpoolmuseums.org.uk/ism

Visit our website for more about the 100 Treasures, and tell us your favourite treasure www.coolcanals.com/100treasures

WILDLIFE HABITAT
"A thing of beauty is a joy forever..."
John Keats (1795-1821)

A transport system built for boats has become a habitat for wildlife too as canals meander the landscape, linking rural and urban Britain. This green corridor is vital as urban development gobbles into green belt, and modern madness gnaws away the English garden in preference of easy maintenance slabs and another house extension. Canals provide an important food source and the banks and verges are a shelter and good breeding area.

Canals are home to an astonishing diversity of life. As well as looking after the canals' built environment for boaters and towpath users, the Canal & River Trust is the guardian of some of Britain's most precious wildlife habitats, and biodiversity has to be planned carefully. The Trust manages the towpath edges to provide shelter for mice, frogs, toads and nesting birds, and the canal banks have to allow clear gaps for water voles to burrow, and keep vegetation protected. Wildlife habitats are affected by every process of a manmade environment - dredging, cutting, building, and the daily impact of boaters and towpath users too.

Wild creatures rely on biodiversity for a sustainable food chain - wild plants, insects, fish, badgers, barn owls, bats, butterflies, water voles, bumblebees, crayfish, dragonflies, rabbits, ladybirds, robins, squirrels, hedgehogs, herons, grass snakes, toads, kingfishers, moorhens, coots, geese, ducks, swans, otters, curlews and countless others. Everyone who visits a canal is sharing the space.

Habitats aren't always obvious (or cute). The brickwork of the canals is home to woodlice, spiders, snails, slugs, flies, millipedes, grasses, lichen and mosses. In the water there are algae, water snails, tadpoles and fish. The trees and hedgerows hide endless species of birds and berries and the surrounding fields are riddled with worms, beetles, moles, badgers, foxes and game.

As seasons change, there's always a new neighbour on the block. The canal is a winter refuge for birds when other waters freeze. Migrating birds such as bitterns and breeding birds such as reed warblers make the canals home for a while. Bats come out to play at dusk and the

ABOVE: A young reed warbler hiding in canalside reeds

sparrows wake up at dawn. On Scottish canals there are buzzards, red squirrels, pine martens, and there's the rare chance of seeing a wild cat or beavers that have recently been reintroduced to the area.

Wildlife is one of the world's natural treasures and protecting wildlife habitats is one of Britain's burning concerns for this century. Canals have a way of simplifying real issues, and every spring, the importance of looking after wildlife habitats tugs the heart strings of little girls and big men, as they both watch with one expression when the first duckling bobs on the water.

ABOVE: Sensitive restoration of the Droitwich Canals has left much of the wildlife habitat intact

WHERE
On canals throughout Britain
The canals are open all day every day - just find your local canal. Spring is of course the best time to see the new baby ducklings, cygnets, goslings and moorhen chicks.

MORE INFO
The Canal & River Trust own or part own over 60 individual Sites of Special Scientific Interest (SSSIs) along the canals of England and Wales. There are a further 9 in Scotland, owned by Scottish Canals.

Canal & River Trust Great Nature Watch (yearly wildlife campaign)

www.canalrivertrust.org.uk www.naturalengland.org.uk www.snh.gov.uk www.ccw.gov.uk

Visit our website for more about the 100 Treasures, and tell us your favourite treasure www.coolcanals.com/100treasures

68 BIRMINGHAM'S HUB
Capital of Britain's canals

London shouts loudest across a nation, but the city of Birmingham can whisper with pride that it is the capital of Britain's canals. The Brummie voice famously chants, "We've got more canals than Venice" and the BCN (Birmingham Canal Navigations) proves it, sprawling the heart of England (without a gondola in sight).

Birmingham is a vibrant multicultural city, bursting at the seams with designer shopping, art galleries, markets and more. And as the city spins its own frenzied delights, an oasis of calm remains quietly hidden away from it all: Brindleyplace is the canal basin tucked right in the city centre. It's where the urban tourist is invited to step into the city's quiet zone, enjoy the balm of water and the laziest bout of slow sightseeing the city can offer.

The hub of the canals offers plenty to see and do, with the waterbus, boat trips, waterside pubs, great places to eat, historic buildings and every consumable pleasure today's traveller might ask for. This retreat from the city can steal a rare moment of silence for the visitor who lets stress sink away in reflections in the water; but, for the sightseer with intent, canal history rumbles fabulously from every nook and cranny, and begs to be explored.

The great spaghetti of canals that converge in Birmingham was once the beating heart of the Industrial Revolution. Cargoes of coal, glass, porcelain, chocolate crumb and the heavy trade of the Black Country were carried by canal boat to and from Birmingham.

The big business of Britain's canals was to link the nation to world markets and in the hot flushes of fierce commercial battles between the canal companies, the daily plight of boat crews sometimes petered into insignificance. Water was precious to competitive canal companies and, in a bid not to lose any of its canal water, the BCN insisted a solid bar was built to separate its canal from the Worcester & Birmingham Canal. The 'Worcester Bar' was built in 1792 and remained in place for 30 years, forcing canal workers to lift cargo over the bar to load and unload clumsily from boat to boat. In 1815, everyone huffed a sigh of relief when a cut was made and the Berlinesque bar was penetrated. The lock has gone, and boats roam freely today, but the bar is still visible to the informed tourist eye.

Gas Street Basin, flowing from Brindleyplace, gives a clue to its importance in its name, as it was the first area in Birmingham to be lit by newfangled gaslights. The neon lights of the modern city reflect a different millennium over Birmingham's canals now, and mark the ever-evolving meeting place of old and new.

WHERE
Birmingham Canal Navigations
Birmingham. OS SP059868

MORE INFO
The National Indoor Arena, the National SEA LIFE Centre and Symphony Hall are all canalside in and around Brindleyplace.

Boat trips and water bus
Catch the water bus or take a boat trip through the heart of Birmingham. www.sherbornewharf.co.uk

Birmingham Tourist Info www.visitbirmingham.com

Visit our website for more about the 100 Treasures, and tell us your favourite treasure www.coolcanals.com/100treasures

RIGHT: Narrowboats in Gas Street Basin overlooked by the ultra-modern Hyatt

69 WEDGWOOD'S CANAL
Pots and philanthropy

An area called the 'Potteries' garlands its skyline with charismatic bottle ovens and chimneys that once, over 200 years ago, puffed pots onto the dining tables of the world. But without the introduction of revolutionary canal routes, mass production would not have been possible in a time before a national transport system. Wedgwood and his factory helped pave the way for that growth in industry as he supported the construction of a canal that was set to deliver to kings and queens, and swamp ordinary households with his innovative hardwearing pots.

Josiah Wedgwood was born in Burslem, Staffordshire, in 1730. His family were potters and he served an apprenticeship with his eldest brother after his father died. As a result of an attack of smallpox as a child, his right leg was weak (which eventually led to a gruesome amputation, without anaesthetic, in 1768) and left Wedgwood less able to perform as a 'thrower' in the pottery works, and so he began modelling instead. The new experience led him to explore more possibilities in the craft, and experiment with different processes. Before long he wanted his own pottery. He opened his first factory in 1759 and his now-famous factory in Etruria in 1766.

Wedgwood's designs were refreshingly simple and durable, attracting royal approval and international popularity. His unglazed blue Jasperware became one of his most recognised designs and his reputation has never faltered since. In 1783, he was elected a fellow of the Royal Society for his pioneering work and his connections with the construction of the Trent & Mersey Canal.

Prior to the arrival of canals, Wedgwood's pots had to be transported in laboriously small quantities by pack horses, clattering along bumpy tracks (with the added hazard of highwaymen and robbers). Boats would be able to carry large loads of mass-produced pots safely, and swiftly.

James Brindley's proposed national canal system would mean Wedgwood's pots could reach ports in Liverpool and Hull, and Wedgwood was keen to support the plan. On June 10 1766, Wedgwood and Brindley attended a meeting in the Crown, a coaching inn at Stone, near Stoke-on-Trent. They discussed the plan to build the 'Grand Trunk' canal (now called the Trent & Mersey) and Wedgwood became treasurer for the project. After the parliamentary bill was presented and authorised, eventually the exciting work could begin.

In his pleasure, in 1766 Wedgwood cut the first sod of earth for the canal and Brindley reputedly carried it away in a barrow! Navvies dug a line out of the earth, 93 miles long, with 76 locks, 5 tunnels, and a climb of 395ft to its summit at Harecastle Tunnel, where the cut burrowed 2880 yards inside a tunnel. It was an extreme engineering achievement to raise the eyebrows of any doubting Thomas. Celebrations were easy to trigger in the euphoria of every step of the progress in the construction, and a grand opening was held when the lock next to the Star pub in Stone was completed. A cannon was fired to mark the jubilation, but in a disastrous calamity it damaged the new lock, which (with red faces!) had to then be rebuilt.

Wedgwood's beloved canal was finally opened in 1777. The Trent & Mersey Canal was a triumph, and so was Wedgwood's factory. When Wedgwood died in 1795, he left his pottery dynasty to his children.

ABOVE: A portrait of Josiah Wedgwood outside the Wedgwood Museum
RIGHT: The Trent & Mersey Canal, a few hundred yards from Wedgwood's factory

Today the great potter is remembered for his creative genius, and Wedgwood pots are still made in Stoke-on-Trent. He is also respected for his philanthropic work. His mother was a Unitarian minister's daughter and Wedgwood never detached ethics from business. His factory made pots, but it also laid a template for a benefits scheme for workers. And, as a vociferous political reformer, Wedgwood passionately supported the abolition of slavery. Wedgwood's life's work wasn't restricted to making pots, his vision and drive influenced the social responsibility of a nation as well.

As the Trent & Mersey Canal quietly ambles through the Potteries today, Wedgwood's life is serenaded in the glorious landscape, and his clay is never far from mind.

WHERE
Trent & Mersey Canal
Stoke-on-Trent. OS SJ887397
The Wedgwood Visitor Centre and Museum are open daily. Factory tours Mar-Oct Mon-Thur. Admission charge. Wedgwood Shop, Museum Shop and Factory Outlet. Café and restaurant. Wheelchair access (apart from the factory tour). Children's play area.

MORE INFO
The Wedgwood Factory, Museum and Visitor Centre are in a huge site covering over 240 acres, bordering the Trent & Mersey Canal. The factory moved here in the early 1930s from its site in Stoke-on-Trent where it had been since the 1700s.

The award-winning Wedgwood Museum has a collection ranging through from the mid-1700s to the present day, including some of the world's finest ceramic examples and Wedgwood's iconic anti-slavery medallion with its image of an enslaved man, and the inscription 'Am I not a Man and a Brother?' It also houses an archive of over 80,000 manuscripts (free to access but you must have a valid 'reader's card' - download the application from their website).

The Visitor Centre runs 'Ceramic Experience Days' which include the opportunity to throw your own pot or paint a plate.

T:01782 282986 www.wedgwoodvisitorcentre.com   T:01782 371919 www.wedgwoodmuseum.org.uk

Visit our website for more about the 100 Treasures, and tell us your favourite treasure www.coolcanals.com/100treasures

70 LLANFOIST WHARF & BLAENAVON
Local people, iron & a World Heritage site that changed the world

Heritage in South Wales comes with lungs full of pride, as honey-sweet voices of male choirs sing from the same hilltops and valleys that once choked children with coal dust from the mines. The story of Blaenavon is a blockbuster on the emotions, with a sweeping landscape that was shaped by the pick and shovel of coal miners, and a town sculpted by its inhabitants, and trade unionists, industrialists, capitalists and eager migrant workers.

Big beautiful Wales is a small country with wide-open panoramas coloured in green and dotted with sheep. But for a time in history, Wales was an industrial nation. Day and night, iron furnaces spat the flames of hell into the sky, in the race to feed the Industrial Revolution. Blaenavon's blessing, and curse, was that it was an area irresistibly rich with limestone, coal and iron ore - all the ingredients needed for successful iron smelting. The Blaenavon works became one of the largest iron smelting works in Britain, and a world leader in the 19th century. The works are now one of Europe's best preserved from the 18th century. The furnaces that were once pioneering in their use of a steam engine instead of water wheels, are now amazing remains that can be seen at the site today.

Transport was the vital key to the success of the area. A tram road built by Thomas Hill, with its tunnel and several inclined planes cascaded down the slopes away from the iron works towards Llanfoist Wharf. The tram road carried bulk from Blaenavon iron works down to the canal at Llanfoist, and here, one single canal boat could carry as much cargo as 200 packhorses, making the canals instrumental in the early achievements of Blaenavon. The canal was originally built as two canals, with the first opening in the late 1700s. After both canals were completed they remained busy until the mid-1800s when the new railways dominated.

Arriving at Llanfoist Wharf today is like discovering an oasis in the middle of the woods. It is a leafy cocoon humming with peace, with only the flight of a dragonfly or the elusive squeak of a resident dormouse to disturb the silence. People come on holiday here now - some hire a narrowboat from Beacon Park boats who are based in the historic wharf, others walk or cycle, or arrive by road just to explore for the day. It's hard, at first glance, to imagine the wharf was once a flurry of less leisurely activity, and to see this canal as a busy export route to Newport. But a walk from Llanfoist, following the old tram roads hidden in the woods up into the mountains is a fascinating trail into Welsh history with a host of heritage clues to be discovered.

The entire length of the Monmouthshire & Brecon Canal today is one of the most scenic in Britain, breathtaking in parts, with views over Pen y Fan and Sugar Loaf Mountain. Its towpath is addictive for walking boots, but the canal around Llanfoist echoes with the excitement of Blaenavon World Heritage Site.

ABOVE: Llanfoist Wharf at the bottom of the tram road from Blaenavon Ironworks, where iron was once loaded onto canal boats

WHERE

Monmouthshire & Brecon Canal
Llanfoist. OS SO284130
Llanfoist Wharf is where the Blaenavon Industrial Landscape UNESCO World Heritage Site meets the canal. The canal is open all day every day. If you cross beneath the canal at the Wharf, it is possible to follow tracks of the former tram roads up into the hills and join the circular Iron Mountain Trail around major industrial sites of the World Heritage Site.

MORE INFO

The bridge and Boathouse at Llanfoist Wharf are both Grade II-listed.

The entire Blaenavon Industrial Landscape is open all day every day, and spreads over approximately 13 square miles. Blaenavon World Heritage Centre is at the heart of the World Heritage Site and gives an overview of its industrial heritage. FREE admission. Tour guides can be booked to take you round the main industrial heritage of the town of Blaenavon. Gift shop and café.

Blaenavon Industrial Landscape UNESCO World Heritage Site includes Big Pit, the National Coal Museum.

T:01495 742333 www.visitblaenavon.co.uk whc.unesco.org/en/list

Visit our website for more about the 100 Treasures, and tell us your favourite treasure www.coolcanals.com/100treasures

71 CANALSIDE TEASHOP
A slice of Victoria sponge and a cuppa

"A cup of tea?" It's a British institution, a holy habit, a cure for all ills. Tea punctuates the day and refreshes the nation; it is served in the living room, in the board room, in hotels, on ocean liners, on building sites and anywhere there are people and a kettle. Yet, few places in Britain can claim the long-time relationship with tea that canals have.

The Cutty Sark launched in 1869 and is the last surviving, and most famous, Tea Clipper in the world (the ship is preserved at Greenwich). Tea that came all the way from China arrived on our shores; and when canals brought chestfuls of luxurious tea inland from the ports of Bristol and Gloucester, an era of posh tea drinking was born in high society. By the mid-1800s afternoon tea was compulsory etiquette, and all aspiring concentric social circles partook!

ABOVE: 'Measham' teapot in the National Waterways Museum. Teapots were ordered by working boatmen on their way through Measham on the Ashby Canal (to be collected on the way back). They were decorated individually and often given for special occasions, then handed down through the generations

Canals didn't just carry cargoes of tea, they also fed the pottery industries of Stoke-on-Trent and Worcester with raw materials to make fine China tea sets, and in turn deliver teapots and teacups to home markets and all across the world. The story of tea has spun from the cups of little finger-cocked crinoline ladies to the big fat mug of builders' brew; and canals have kept up with the times. Today, wherever tourists go, there is usually a teashop with a 'ready to whistle' kettle: and the canalside teashop serves a cuppa with both pride and ambience. Whether the leisure seeker cares about the heritage of tea on the canals or not, the joy of sipping a relaxing cup of tea on the water's edge, with boats and ducks and the slow sounds of summer for company, is one of life's rare peaceful pleasures.

Historic lockkeepers' cottages, stables and store rooms have often been transformed into tearooms. There are floating teashops too, on narrowboats and barges. Some tearooms have staff dressed in traditional canal clothes offering nostalgic doily frills, others prefer chic designer minimalism or a cosy cluttered welcome. Across the canal networks every teashop is individual and inseparable from its environment. The teashop on the Caledonian Canal with Neptune's Staircase and Ben Nevis in view, is a different experience to the lockside tearoom overlooking Trent Lock and the dramatic chimneys of Ratcliffe Power Station, and a view over Sowerby Bridge Wharf has different riches to Brecon in Wales or the canal in Camden.

Whether you seek out your local teashop on a canal nearby, or travel to a canal far away, nothing can reach in and throw the knots of stress away better than a wedge of home-baked Victoria Sponge, served with a piping hot brew.

WHERE
On canals throughout Britain
The canals are open all day every day - just find your local canal.

MORE INFO
Full listings of all canalside teashops in Britain can be found in our online directory. www.coolcanals.com

---

Visit our website for more about the 100 Treasures, and tell us your favourite treasure www.coolcanals.com/100treasures

RIGHT: Tea and cake with a boaty view at Kizzie's on the Oxford Canal

72 GRAHAM PALMER STONE
One of the canal heroes

Over 200 years ago the unknown navvy was sent scrambling across every corner of Britain to cut thousands of miles of ditches out of the land with his humble shovel. His ditches were filled with water and hailed as the masterworks of great engineers. That era of Canal Mania paid no homage to the nameless navvy. His job was servile and uncouth, a mere tool for the mighty Empire that employed him (for a pittance). Around 200 years later, Graham Palmer (who died tragically young in 1988) redefined the status of digging dirt from the ground, when he became the father of the modern day navvy. He took up the baton of helping to restore some of Britain's lost and decaying canals under the flag of Waterway Recovery Group (WRG).

The roots of the WRG gathered momentum in 1969 on the 'Big Dig Weekend', when around 300 people cleared a section of the Montgomery Canal through Welshpool. Graham Palmer saw the need to coordinate willing volunteers into the most worthwhile restoration projects - and formed the WRG in 1970. WRG evolved and made the job description of a modern day navvy sound like occupational fun. Graham Palmer's work didn't end when he died - the WRG remains dedicated to the tasks ahead. The famous red T-shirts of WRG became the attention-grabbing colour behind the setting up of the annual Inland Waterways Association (IWA) festival site. And anyone can join in and go on one of their famous working camps, affectionately known as a 'Dirty Weekend'. A good time is guaranteed, as well as the sense of achievement from the new skills a volunteer gains from mucking in with a team. One of the WRG's largest restoration projects has been the rebuilding of the four Frankton Locks and three Aston Locks on the Montgomery Canal, and most recently it helped in the restoration and reopening in 2012 of the Droitwich Canals.

On the 40th anniversary of the 'Big Dig Weekend', a memorial stone was erected on the Montgomery Canal (to replace a former stone). The success of WRG lies in the chiselled face of Graham Palmer on an unshielded stone. Passersby can share a moment in the company of a canal hero - with a soundtrack of water trickling into the lock, as if to herald his achievements and the movement he founded.

Graham is immortalised on the beautiful canal that carves its way through Wales. His chiselled stone face is worn, but never looks weary as he watches over his lock (named after him). Almost symbolically, his memorial stone is destined to decay, just as the canals he loved did - and there's a peacefulness that surrounds this uplifting spot on the Monty, as if Graham Palmer earned his place in the timeline of Britain's canals and he fits here. A canal lined with oaks and old buildings curling into the landscape mingles with the sweetest smells of Wales for pure joy. The oaks ask you to linger and the canal rolling into the hills ahead calls you onwards. Thanks to the help of people like Graham Palmer, you have the choice.

WHERE
Montgomery Canal
Near Lower Frankton. OS SJ366309
The stone stands alongside Graham Palmer Lock, just beyond bridge 71.

MORE INFO
The Waterway Recovery Group was originally formed as an independent body, but now operates as a division of the Inland Waterways Association. They are always looking for new volunteers, and there are many ways to get involved - helping out at canal restoration camps and 'dirty weekends', digging, building locks, or even being the canal camp cook...

Waterway Recovery Group www.wrg.org.uk   www.waterways.org.uk

---

Visit our website for more about the 100 Treasures, and tell us your favourite treasure www.coolcanals.com/100treasures

RIGHT: Graham Palmer's stone

GRAHAM PALMER

FOUNDER OF

THE

WATERWAY RECOVERY

GROUP

My favourite treasure - chosen and written by Peter Collins:
Collections Manager at the National Waterways Museum

" **Choosing one object from the collection is a very difficult task as there are so many items in the collection that have historical, social and cultural significance - when you take into account that the collection includes documents, books, images, engines and 3-D objects that illustrate the story of the canals over the last 250 years or so.**

However when one has to choose, I have gone for the narrowboat Mendip as, through its extensive history, it incorporates so many items from across the collection.

Mendip was built in Northwich by Yarwood & Sons in 1948 for Fellows Morton & Clayton and later became owned by British Waterways (now the Canal & River Trust). Mendip carried many cargoes over its service but its most famous was chocolate crumb for Cadbury, with its main skipper Charlie Atkins becoming known as 'Chocolate Charlie' and a well-known character on the canal network.

Mendip's history is told in the Museum through images, documents, artwork and books which all help tell the story of this important narrowboat's exploits with Charlie. In 2011 Mendip recreated its chocolate crumb journey to Bournville from the National Waterways Museum after it was restored, funded by support from Cadbury, in the Museum's Heritage Boatyard. "
PETER COLLINS

ABOVE: Mendip moored up during the 2011 recreation of the chocolate journey
RIGHT: Mendip being restored in 2010 in the Heritage Boatyard at the National Waterways Museum

WHERE
Shropshire Union Canal
Ellesmere Port. OS SJ405771
Mendip is on display in the National Waterways Museum in Ellesmere Port. Open daily. Café and gift shop. Admission charge. Wheelchair access to most areas.

T:0151 3555017 www.nwm.org.uk

MORE INFO
Mendip is listed on the National Register of Historic Vessels (NRHV).

www.nationalhistoricships.org.uk

Visit our website for more about the 100 Treasures, and tell us your favourite treasure www.coolcanals.com/100treasures

Bingley is a factory town, famous for thermal underwear; yet more spectacularly, sitting on the edge of town, it hides a howling treasure of Britain's canals that plays with the fears of the water traveller. This is Yorkshire, and a tough spirit is needed to conquer this 60ft canal climb: Bingley Five-Rise is the steepest lock staircase in Britain. It is the horrible, thrilling, perfect boat ride for the adrenalin junkie - keeping the richest rewards for those who dare.

The staircase locks were built in 1774, and worn cobbled brickwork snuggles, without fuss, into a beefy canal scene that is heavy with heritage. Boats tackle the staircase with ginger care today, but the working boats of the past had tight delivery schedules to meet and couldn't pamper to fears for safety.

The boater has to face a chilling ride, with all the locks joined together in a staircase (rather than having the more usual space in between). Each lock opens straight into the next one, creating a precipitous climb with deathly gallons of water looming behind the gates above every lock the boat clambers up through. Heading downhill, vertigo takes over with the daunting feeling of a cliff edge. Mid-flight the thunder of water tells you there's no turning back. There's no room for errors in the precision exercise of filling and emptying the chambers to carry boats up or down the flight. This is canal drama at its best, with a guaranteed mix of feisty engineering, boat handling skills, extreme gongoozling and the genuine smiles of a shared experience.

ABOVE: The view from the top of the Five-Rise Locks

The old stables at the top of the staircase locks have been converted into a teashop, serving refreshments to boaters in need of Dutch courage, and to towpath visitors just to add to the fun of it all.

By boat and by towpath, Bingley Five-Rise Locks is awesome. It's said that over 30,000 people turned up to celebrate its opening in 1774, and in 2012 it didn't even need water to attract visitors. Over 7,000 people turned up and queued to see the locks on a cold weekend in January 2012, when it had been drained to allow engineers to replace the old gates. With the terror of the water harnessed, visitors were allowed to clamber down scaffolded steps to get a different view of the locks. From the canal bed the monster gates made mice out of men, and filled everyone up with respect for canal engineers past and present. The gates were replaced at a cost of £200,000 and in 25 years the job will be repeated again. The dedication, and colossal cost, of keeping this treasure open for navigation is testament to its worth.

ABOVE: The impressive sight of Bingley Five-Rise Locks

WHERE
Leeds & Liverpool Canal
Bingley. OS SE107399

MORE INFO
The locks remain virtually unaltered since they were first built in 1774 by local stonemasons to a design by John Longbotham. There's a view from the top over Bingley's mills and the hills beyond, and a well-placed café (the former stables) at the top. A few hundred yards further along the canal below the Five-Rise Locks are Bingley's Three-Rise Locks, a less dramatic version of the five.

Bingley Five-Rise Locks are one of the greatest engineering feats of the canal age. The steepest lock staircase in Britain, it is Grade I-listed, and was awarded a Transport Trust Red Wheel Plaque (the first one in Yorkshire) in 2010.

www.transporttrust.com   www.transportheritage.com

Visit our website for more about the 100 Treasures, and tell us your favourite treasure www.coolcanals.com/100treasures

75 BRAUNSTON VILLAGE
A canal parish

Britain's canals link city to city, meandering through open green countryside in between. The roving networks create a linear floating village where people connect and nod hello. Canals are all about travel, and relationships (by necessity) are formed quickly with passing strangers. Sometimes canal hubs develop with static clusters of boats and buildings that spread out on the canalside. Braunston is a canal village huddled in the best countryside of Northamptonshire.

The canals only arrived in Braunston in the 1700s, but the Doomsday Book refers to a settlement here known as Brandestone. Seriously old hawthorn hedgerows bellow with pagan thorns and blossom, and the map is sprinkled with medieval sites.

Braunston today has all it needs to ooze quintessential English charm. There's a teashop, pubs, little stone cottages, and the old bakery even hangs a 'Hovis' sign to waft imaginary smells of bread from a retired oven, baked of course with flour ground in the old windmill next door to the church on the hill. The bricks and mortar do their best, but something in the air says the 'real' village of Braunston is in the hubbub around the marina.

The marina sits near the junction of the Grand Union and Oxford Canals, which was once one of the busiest commercial trading points linking with London. Leisure boats own the water now, and Braunston has become a photogenic hotspot for holidaymakers, with Horseley iron bridges, historic workshops, and a marina bobbing with narrowboats of all colours.

The spire of All Saints Church guards over the village, just as it has for generations of boating families who have passed through ever since the first working boats. It is known as the boatman's church since it has christened and married many from the floating community. And the graves of boaters lie here too. The church is much loved by its canal community, and Braunston's lively vicar can't help but be involved with the canal population. TV has had 'An Island Parish' and 'A Seaside Parish', and Braunston would fit the real life version of 'A Canal Parish'. It's not just the village, it's the people who live there, and who travel through, who make it Braunston.

WHERE
Grand Union Canal
Braunston. OS SP540658

MORE INFO
A photogenic Grade II-listed double cast-iron bridge spans the junction where the Grand Union Canal meets the Oxford Canal at Braunston Turn, and further along the canal Braunston's marina has mooring for up to 250 boats, buys and sells new and used boats, has two dry docks and a collection of historic buildings housing everything from rope to magazines.

Next to the bottom of Braunston's flight of locks is a tiny bookshop which prides itself on having one of the largest collections of canal-related books in the country. It also sells canal giftware and of course ice-creams.

www.boatshopbraunston.co.uk

Historic Working Boat Rally
Time your visit to Braunston for the annual boat rally at the end of June - it's the largest gathering of traditional working boats which pack together along the canal in a colourful procession of heritage.

www.braunstonmarina.co.uk www.braunston.org.uk

Visit our website for more about the 100 Treasures, and tell us your favourite treasure www.coolcanals.com/100treasures

RIGHT: Double cast-iron bridge (made at Horseley Ironworks in Tipton) at the junction of the Grand Union and Oxford Canals

HORSE BOAT
The power that drove the Industrial Revolution

Real horse power was the energy of an Empire before the engine was invented. Most canal boats were towed by heavy horses and managed to top 2 miles per hour when a narrowboat was loaded, and 3 miles per hour when unladen. Two centuries have passed, and the rules of speed have changed in the haulage industry, letting the dust settle on the towpaths where those heroes of the canals once trod.

A traditional boat horse was expected to do a working class job that was sweaty and often grizzly, and his, or her, reward was a respected place in the team that crewed a working boat. Boat crews would majestically adorn their horses' bridles, nosebags and any available paraphernalia, with brightly coloured canal art. Decoration of roses and castles didn't make his task any lighter, but it has left a romantic image for the story of the canals.

The rules of the road were few, but strict. Loaded boats had priority and when horses passed in opposite directions, one boatman had to drop the towrope to let the other horse step past. The traditional haulage business of working horses on the canals has gone, but the gentle souls of giant horses leave their legacy in the trust of new generations who can learn the skills of horseboating. There can't be a single iconic sight that sums up the nostalgia, power and purpose of Britain's canals better than a heavy horse gently towing a boatful of people along a canal today. It is a rare chance to see horseboating in action these days, with only a handful of horse boats still operating. Sue Day is the champion of the Horseboating Society, with a big reputation for her passion for passing on the skills and traditions of horseboating to future generations. She turns up with her steedy companions at waterways festivals and events across the networks, and beacons the cause of her tremendously important society.

And the beautiful spirits of horses that once clopped rhythmically along the towpaths of the Industrial Revolution secretly conceal their epitaph in rope marks gouged under bridges, and waterside stables that have been converted. Horses are a living treasure of the canals to honour, love and respect.

ABOVE: Horse-drawn boat trip on the Llangollen Canal
LEFT: Horse-drawn boat at Tiverton on the Grand Western Canal

LOCATION

Grand Western Canal, Kennet & Avon Canal, Llangollen Canal and the river Wey Navigations

MORE INFO

There are only four horseboat companies still operating in the UK - at Godalming in Surrey, Hungerford in Berkshire, Llangollen in Wales and Tiverton in Devon. They all offer horse-drawn boat trips during the summer season.

Godalming Packetboat Company www.horseboat.org.uk
Kennet Horse Boat Company www.kennet-horse-boat.co.uk
Welsh Canal Holiday Craft www.horsedrawnboats.co.uk
Tiverton Canal Company www.tivertoncanal.co.uk

The Horseboating Society works to promote horseboating and preserve its heritage and skills. www.horseboating.org.uk

Working horses, mules and donkeys in some of the poorest countries of the world can suffer unnecessary hardships. The Brooke is a charity that aims to improve the lives and welfare of these working animals. www.thebrooke.org

Visit our website for more about the 100 Treasures, and tell us your favourite treasure www.coolcanals.com/100treasures

My favourite treasures - chosen and written by Nigel Crowe:
Head of Heritage for the Canal & River Trust

❝ The rattle of paddle gear is one of the classic sounds of summer.

It typically consists of a hand-worked iron rack and pinion mechanism that raises and lowers a paddle across the mouth of a culvert or an opening in a gate to let water into and out of a lock chamber. Paddle gear is found up and down the country and comes in many shapes and styles. This historic diversity owed much to individual canal companies. In modern times old company styles became diluted, but many local variations survive today.

Early paddle gear on river navigations, none of which survives in use, was gate mounted and was usually of the wooden peg-and-pull type. The more familiar cast iron rack and pinion gear was a largely 18th-century innovation which has remained in use for at least two hundred years.

Paddle gear components wear out and need replacing at intervals. Replacement parts can be fabricated or made from casting moulds, some of which are historic and still bear the name of an original canal company. Birmingham Canal Navigations (BCN) ground paddle gear mounted on inscribed cast-iron jacks is a commonly occurring type on Midlands canals. Rarer varieties include ball and chain counterweighted gears on the Bridgwater & Taunton Canal, handspike sets on the Calder & Hebble Navigation and extraordinary reversed incline ground paddle gears on the Oxford Canal at Hillmorton that originally date from the mid-19th century.

The 20th century has left its own examples, not least of which are the 'candlesticks' on the 1920s and 1930s sections of the Grand Union Canal, still in daily use and installed when the country was going through one of the worst recessions in its history. Even the 1970s 'granny paddles' which were hydraulically worked, now have a certain nostalgia about them. ❞
NIGEL CROWE

WHERE
On canals throughout Britain
The canals are open all day every day - just find your local canal.

MORE INFO
Examples of historic paddle gear can be seen in the National Waterways Museum at Ellesmere Port, and in other waterways museums such as Gloucester, London and Stoke Bruerne.

www.nwm.org.uk www.gloucesterwaterwaysmuseum.org.uk www.stokebruernecanalmuseum.org.uk

Visit our website for more about the 100 Treasures, and tell us your favourite treasure www.coolcanals.com/100treasures

RIGHT: Unusual ball and chain mechanism on the Bridgwater & Taunton Canal's locks

78 SKIPTON BASIN
The Gateway to the Dales

The Yorkshire Dales are the prized hiking haven for woolly hats and walkers at the heart of the Pennines. They are also where boaters can cruise one of Britain's most extreme canals, the Leeds & Liverpool. Perched on the edge of the National Park, the tiny characterful town of Skipton is known as the Gateway to the Dales with the canal running straight through the centre.

Skipton wasn't discovered by the canal builders, its heritage reels back as far as the 7th century when Saxon farmers called it 'Sheep Town'. Its peace and quiet was butted aside when the war-mongering Normans built a castle in the 12th century. The castle still stands looking over the High Street and the canal, but battles are thankfully kept in the past. It's claimed that the fortress that can be seen today is one of England's best preserved, all thanks to Lady Anne Clifford who, in the 17th century, rebuilt some sections.

Out of site of Skipton, there's a nearby quarry with lorries that trot to and fro, but the old quarry once used a horse tramway that ran all the way to the castle. There, chutes were used to drop quarried rock into boats to be carried on the Leeds & Liverpool Canal.

Today, Skipton's clean air, cobbled streets, Georgian houses, brightly coloured narrowboats, markets and fairs have become its attraction. Skipton has been a hive of activity on market days ever since Norman times and tourists bulk the crowds who amble around the canal basin. The canal was originally an addition to the town as a commercial transport route; today it adds boaty charm and unrivalled appeal that makes it one of the Dales' most charismatic towns.

The Leeds & Liverpool Canal strolls away from town in two directions - both venture into some of the most uplifting countryside anywhere on England's canals. The charm of Skipton is only rivalled by the temptation to keep following the canal.

WHERE
Leeds & Liverpool Canal
Skipton. OS SD987516
The canal basin is in the heart of Skipton. It's a hub of activity with boats, cyclists and walkers, and of course gongoozlers.

MORE INFO
Boat trips & dayboat hire
From Skipton Basin, boat trips take you along the Springs Branch of the canal beneath Skipton Castle (the 900-year-old castle is one of the best preserved medieval castles in England), or along the main Leeds & Liverpool Canal. Alternatively you can hire a self-drive dayboat.

www.canaltrips.co.uk www.penninecruisers.com www.airedalecruising.info

Skipton Tourist Info
www.skiptononline.co.uk

Visit our website for more about the 100 Treasures, and tell us your favourite treasure www.coolcanals.com/100treasures

RIGHT: The entrance to the Springs Branch off Skipton Basin

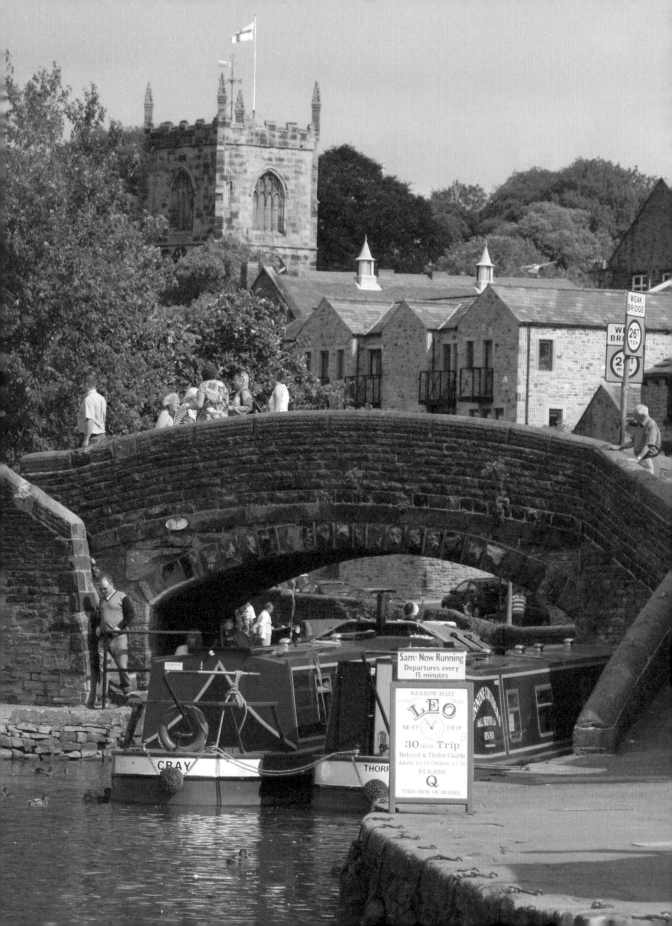

The canal lock is a masterpiece of simplicity that ingeniously carries boats uphill and downhill in still water. It's the place gongoozlers gather and where passing boats cram conversations and camaraderie as they wait for their boats to be lifted from one water level to another. The ordinary lock is the humble showpiece of Britain's entire canal system. Without it, canals wouldn't work.

Any canal journey would have ended at the first incline, since without nature's tides or currents, the water in manmade canals wouldn't allow canal boats to travel up or downhill without help. A lock is a manmade chamber with wooden or steel gates at either end. In canal terms, it creates the 'pound' between a canal that is split on a slope, at two flat levels. A boat that wants to travel uphill through a lock must empty the water from the chamber to match the level of the lower canal. The bottom gates can then be opened, and the boat enters the chamber. By using a windlass to turn the top paddle, a sluice gate opens and allows water to fill the chamber from the upper canal. The gates are held shut by the pressure of water, and it is only when the level reaches the same height as the upper canal that the top gate can be opened, and the boat can carry on its journey. A boat wanting to travel downhill follows the same process in reverse.

The working lock has no need for improvement, its simplicity is its joy, and everyone who sets off on a canal journey today becomes a time traveller, working the locks in the same way as they would have functioned over 200 years ago. But the canal lock has older roots than 19th-century Britain. It is believed that Chhiao Wei-Yo invented the pound lock in AD983, with the first recorded lock built on China's Grand Canal in AD984. Two water gates were built 250ft apart to create a temporary alteration in the water levels. Italy is recorded to have been the first to introduce the true pound lock in 1373, a century before Britain dabbled

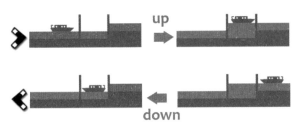

with the idea. And with its vertical gates and pioneering spirit, the Exeter Ship Canal was responsible for the first pound lock in Britain. The mitre lock with its familiar v-shaped gates which are held together by the physics of water dates back to Leonardo Da Vinci (1452-1519). Britain's first mitre lock was on the River Lee at Waltham Abbey.

The ordinary lock is historic, but if history implies something past, the canal lock is much more than that. Canals keep reinventing themselves, with new water travellers arriving with every era. From traditional 19th-century working boats, to the Idle Women doing their bit for World War II, and from the pioneering leisure boaters of post-war times to the Canal Mania of recent years: the humble lock has served them all.

Its function is the undeniable triumph of Britain's canal networks, yet more unquantifiably the visual dynamics of entire canalscapes owe everything to the lock. The vision of great outstretched arms that are coated in the distinctive, and oddly romantic, black and white colours of the Canal & River Trust does more than anything else to pump the adrenalin of a view.

Some folk might head off to sightsee the biggest lock flight in the most spectacular scenery, others may simply saunter to their local canal, but everyone inevitably ends up standing and staring, trying to unravel the unfathomable mystery, 'how does a lock work?'

ABOVE: Audlem Lock Flight on the Shropshire Union Canal

WHERE

On canals throughout Britain

The canals are open all day every day - just find your local canal.

The longest lock flight in Britain is at Tardebigge on the Worcester & Birmingham Canal, the deepest lock is Tuel Lane Lock at Sowerby Bridge on the Rochdale Canal, the steepest staircase of locks is Bingley Five Rise on the Leeds & Liverpool Canal, and the longest staircase is the Caen Hill Flight at Devizes on the Kennet & Avon Canal.

MORE INFO

There are two different types of single locks. The broad lock can hold wider boats or can fit two narrowboats side by side, and the narrow lock can only fit one narrowboat at a time. Some of the wonders of the waterways come from individual locks being joined together as a long flight or a steep staircase - or when they appear in unusual locations, opening into the sea, or are built to be extra deep or wide due to the terrain.

Visit our website for more about the 100 Treasures, and tell us your favourite treasure www.coolcanals.com/100treasures

My favourite treasures - chosen and written by Nigel Crowe:
Head of Heritage for the Canal & River Trust

> **Kilns were once a common canalside feature and their half-buried remains can still be discovered at hundreds of sites up and down the canals of England and Wales.**

In some places whole banks of kilns were built to serve industrial brickyards and limeworks where clay and limestone were processed and fired to produce bricks and quicklime. These kilns were generally placed as close to the water as possible to allow the movement of raw materials and finished products by boat.

The Monmouthshire & Brecon and Montgomery Canals, which were constructed to serve their local agricultural industries, are rich in the remains of lime kilns. Some of their kiln-banks have great archaeological interest and are scheduled monuments or listed buildings. Old maps of the Birmingham Canal Navigations are peppered with kilns of all sorts and dozens of former brick kiln sites dot the banks of canals like the Grand Union, Kennet & Avon and Oxford.

The downdraught type brick kiln which still stands on the Oxford Canal at Fenny Compton is typical of many that have now vanished. A brickyard was established here in the 1840s and the kiln was probably built sometime afterwards. It was active until 1917, firing bricks and drainpipes for the Oxford Canal Company. In World War II, it saw service as a poultry shed-cum-air raid shelter and a drawing of 1954 shows it in use as a hay store. Today it has been cleared of vegetation and repaired by volunteers and if you're passing Fenny Compton, it is well worth a visit.
NIGEL CROWE

WHERE
Scattered on canals across Britain

MORE INFO
The canals are open all day every day - just find your local canal.

RIGHT: Lime kilns at Llangattock Wharf on the
Monmouthshire & Brecon Canal

GHOST
Hunt out the most haunted places on the canals... if you dare

In the language of tourism, the canals of Britain are havens of heavenly bliss that help cleanse the soul... but that's not the whole story! Canals have another, darker tale to tell - one that unravels ghoulish reports of grisly happenings and ghostly sightings (irresistible fun for ghost-busting kids and grownups with the devil in them)

Rumour has it that the most haunted canal in England is the Shropshire Union Canal. It was built in the 19th century and runs from Autherley Junction near Wolverhampton to Ellesmere Port in Cheshire. Its spooky reputation is probably due to the shadowy sections that cut deeply through long straight embankments.

But whether the water-road takes a straight course across Shropshire, or weaves under trip-trap bridges in Wales, or tiptoes into dark tunnels in the North, canals everywhere are apparently riddled with cackling horrors. Of course any sceptic worth his salt would have nothing to do with such stuff-and-nonsense; but all travellers who find themselves gobbled up by the darkness of a 'reputedly' haunted canal tunnel, can only emerge the other side secretly breathing a light sigh of relief. Tunnels play tricks with the sanest of minds, as sounds echo and inescapable smells bellow with dank demons. Only the pinhead of light ahead can keep hope alive.

Kit Crewbucket is one of the most famous devilish divas to haunt the canals. Poor old Kit was murdered and her headless corpse was dumped in the canal. Her ghost has taken up residence on the Trent & Mersey Canal ever since, with wails that are said to bounce through Harecastle Tunnel. Big burly boatmen working on the canal in the 19th century would prefer to take a ludicrously long detour rather than face the hideous journey through Harecastle Tunnel (big burly boatmen cruising the canals today might too!)

The saga of the 'Bloody Steps' is another famous story to keep white-faced canal tourists entertained. In 1839, on the canal at Brindley Bank near Rugeley in Staffordshire, Christina Collins was tragically murdered. As her body was dragged from the water, blood ran down a flight of steps from the canal and it is reported that the stain sometimes reappears as Christina haunts the spot.

But it's not just the English who fall for the follies and frights of ghosts, even brave Scotland can be secretly superstitious, as its canals cling on to Celtic traditions for protection. The rowan is a common sight on the canalside in the Highlands, and steedy canal workers might still find comfort in the old tree folklore that claims the rowan gives protection against evil.

Hunting down the best ghosts of the cut can be tourism with a twist, taking you to unusual and interesting places you've never been before. But ghost hunting doesn't have to be hard work - the best place for a good yarn is to pop into your local canal pub. They're bound to claim to have a resident ghost. For over 200 years, from drunken navvies who first built the canals, to the happy holidaymaker today, the canalside pub has been the place where ghosts are frequently seen. And pubs that coincidentally serve very good ale, often keep the merriest spectres of all (it's surprisingly good for trade).

ABOVE: The entrance to Blisworth Tunnel at Stoke Bruerne on the Grand Union Canal. Halfway through the tunnel, a mysterious candlelit phantom tunnel appears - reputedly on the spot where a rock fall in the late 18th century killed 14 navvies as they worked by candlelight

LIMEHOUSE BASIN
The world's gateway to inland Britain

Its name comes from Les Lymhoost, the 14th-century lime kilns on the river, and its fame comes from its service to an Empire. Limehouse Basin links the Regent's Canal to the River Thames; and when it opened in 1820, it was the world's gateway to over 2,000 miles of inland waterways reaching across Britain - and it is still fabulously navigable today.

London's Docklands, and the stylish Canary Wharf with its beanstalk offices, peep over the shoulder of Limehouse Basin. It's a skyline that shares a goose-bumped history of oceangoing vessels arriving with new exotic fruits and fancies from faraway places.

At Limehouse Basin, goods were loaded and unloaded to and from smaller boats that could travel along the canals that linked London to Birmingham. The Basin doesn't dress up and pretend to be a tourist hotspot, but it attracts wide-eyed travellers with its own version of an East End drama.

Limehouse was the first China Town in London, and in Victorian times it became a notorious den for opium and illegal gambling. Just off the canal, a short walk from Limehouse Basin, the Ragged School Museum is the place to see how the Victorians educated their East End children. It was once the largest Ragged (free) school and was set up by Dr Barnardo.

When the Docklands closed in the 1960s, Limehouse Basin had to find new purpose. In an amazing transformation, the area is now stylish glass and steel waterside living, with pubs and cafés. A ninety-berth marina adds authenticity and interest to the water and the tidal Thames is told to behave itself beyond the basin.

LOCATION
Regent's Canal
London. OS TQ363809

MORE INFO
Limehouse Basin used to be known as Regent's Canal Dock. In one corner, the Regent's Canal leaves the Basin heading north and then west past Hoxton, King's Cross, Camden and Regent's Park to join the Grand Union Canal Paddington Arm at Little Venice, before eventually joining the Grand Union Canal main line at Bull's Bridge and heading north towards Birmingham & the Midlands.

In the other corner of the Basin, the Limehouse Cut creates a short cut to the Lee Navigation, one of the routes to the Olympic Park used by the 'Water Chariots' waterbus during the 2012 Olympics.

www.water-chariots.co.uk

Take a wander around Limehouse Basin and down to where it meets the Thames. One of the oldest pubs in London overlooks the river there - Charles Dickens was a patron and wrote about it in 'Our Mutual Friend'.

Visit our website for more about the 100 Treasures, and tell us your favourite treasure www.coolcanals.com/100treasures

RIGHT: Limehouse Basin is overlooked by Canary Wharf

My favourite treasures - chosen and written by Nigel Crowe:
Head of Heritage for the Canal & River Trust

" **It is popular myth that gates on old locks are sometimes original. They are not. A 200-year-old lock may have been re-gated half a dozen or more times in its lifetime.**

And while the design of each gate remained firmly within established carpentry traditions, its finished appearance was often subtly different to the one it replaced. Beam ends, grab handles, footplates and stirrups, L's and T's (the iron and later steel strengthening pieces) have appeared, vanished and then reappeared over time. These subtle differences are part of the appeal of the working heritage of the waterways.

The Canal & River Trust is very good at designing and building lock gates and in general, traditional patterns and details are still followed. The traditional material for lock gates is English oak, although exotic timber like jarrah and ekki and opepe was sometimes used in the 20th century before questions about sustainability and tropical hardwoods came to the fore. Other variations included steel gates and composite (steel and wood) gates.

Rarest of all surviving materials is iron. Incredibly, there are still mid-19th century cast-iron lock gates on the Oxford Canal at Claydon and at Hillmorton Locks on the edge of Rugby where a pair of bottom gates were repaired and replaced just a few years ago. The gates are the bottom set on the offside chamber of the Middle Locks on this interesting paired formation that was part of the Oxford Canal Company's 'modernisation' programme of the 1840s. The Bottom Lock chamber on the towpath side also has a cast-iron top gate, with a sailor's hat strapping post. "

NIGEL CROWE

WHERE
On canals throughout Britain
The canals are open all day every day - just find your local canal.

MORE INFO
The Canal & River Trust often need to change or repair lock gates during their winter maintenance programme - it is sometimes possible to watch them at work.

For more information, visit their website www.canalandrivertrust.org.uk

Visit our website for more about the 100 Treasures, and tell us your favourite treasure www.coolcanals.com/100treasures

RIGHT: Old lock gates piled up at the lockside on the newly restored Droitwich Canal

Falkirk did the impossible when it grabbed an old cliché and really did 'reinvent the wheel'. This unassuming patch in Scotland gave the globe a wheel of monumental structure - a masterpiece to commemorate the modernity of Britain's canals in this Millennium. When Her Majesty The Queen turned up to open the Falkirk Wheel in 2002, she unveiled the world's first rotating Boat Lift.

No one knows exactly when mankind first invented the wheel, but it was unarguably one of the most vital human discoveries. Ancient history tells us potters were using wheels by 3500BC and Sumeria used wheeled vehicles soon after. The wheel became the basis of travel - and today, at Falkirk, even a boat needs a wheel if it is to venture the impossible 115ft gap between the Forth & Clyde Canal and the Union Canal.

The two canals were once linked by a flight of eleven locks at Falkirk, but these were closed and dismantled in 1933. From then on, boats were left to simply 'mind the gap'. That was until the ambitious plan by British Waterways (now Scottish Canals in Scotland, Canal & River Trust in England and Wales) to rebuild a link unbridled the passions of designers and architects.

A mad melting pot of ferocious fundraising, art and invention led to the phenomenal success of the Falkirk Wheel. The project cost £17.5 million and it took over 1,000 craftsmen and over 1,200 tons of steel to build the wheel. The structure was first assembled at Butterley Engineering's steelworks. Then it was dismantled and taken by a fleet of 35 lorries to Falkirk to be built on site. After 14,000 bolts had been tightened by hand, the wheel was ready to go to work.

How the wheel works is mysteriously simple. There are two gondolas full of water, one at the upper level and one at the lower level, and when a canal boat enters the upper gondola to be lowered to the basin below, the lower gondola simultaneously rises. The elementary physics of the process echo Archimedes' 'principle of displacement'. When a boat enters a gondola that is full of water, it spills water and the remaining total mass of the gondola and the boat always balances the same weight. Cogs and wheels give the gondolas a smooth ride up and down. The giant wheel stands 115ft tall and yet uses a mouse-sized 1.5KWh of energy to turn. Ten hydraulic motors in the central spine of the wheel provide the electricity needed to turn the wheel.

The lift takes 15 minutes to rise, and travellers then follow a route through the 590ft Roughcastle Tunnel under the historic Antonine Wall. After a descent on the Wheel, there's a visitor centre in the basin where you can take as much time as you like exploring.

Scotland's heritage is riddled with tartan bravery, and the arrival of the Falkirk Wheel holds echoes of wild cries and a gutsy landscape. It has become a top tourist attraction with over half a million people who pilgrim each year to witness the meeting of two historic canals in the hands of this millennium's marvel.

WHERE
Forth & Clyde / Union Canals
Falkirk OS NS852801
Open daily. Entry FREE to Visitor Centre, grounds, café & gift shop. Charge for boat trips. Wheelchair access. Water Activity Zone beneath the Wheel, children's play park and nature trail, woodland walks and cycle hire.

MORE INFO
Boat Trip
The Falkirk Wheel makes enough of a statement from the ground but take a 50-minute boat trip and get a boat's eye view from inside the wheel. Two glass-topped trip boats, 'Antonine' and 'Archimedes', take you on the journey between the Forth & Clyde Canal and the Union Canal above.

One of the modern wonders of the waterways.

T:08700 500208 www.thefalkirkwheel.co.uk

Visit Scottish Canals for more info about the canal. www.scottishcanals.co.uk

Visit our website for more about the 100 Treasures, and tell us your favourite treasure www.coolcanals.com/100treasures

85 TOWPATH
Trekking across a nation

'Canals are for boats' is the 200-year-old mantra that chants as freshly as ever. If historic water routes become unnavigable, they lose integrity and life. It's boats and boaters that create the colour and fascination everyone who visits canals wants to see, but without towpaths canals would never work.

Canals arrived before the engine was invented and boats were originally pulled by horses. Heavy hoof prints on the towpath said the towpath wasn't a place for leisure or pleasure, and woe betide anyone who got in the way.

The Victorians were serial strollers, they loved promenades and piers and devoured flat straight parkways and crescents. They indulged themselves with a pastime that could have taken them to miles of stunningly beautiful towpath trails, yet no one strolled along canal towpaths for fun in Victorian times. Canals were work places, where filth was rife and dastardly deeds and shenanigans went on. Specially ornate bridges, such as those designed by John Rennie in Bath, might entice a lady to reluctantly cross the canal in order to reach more pleasant city parks, but to choose to walk with canal folk and their belching boats would have been preposterous.

After the railways arrived, and canal companies abandoned the canals, many towpaths became overgrown through years of neglect; and it wasn't until the regeneration of urban waterside areas and the clearing programme of British Waterways (now Canal & River Trust) that mile upon mile of towpaths were open again. Towpaths now scramble from Cornwall to Scotland, over Welsh mountains, the Pennines, through Areas of Outstanding Natural Beauty (AONB), and almost every city in Britain. Wherever the canal dares to go, the towpath will follow. The slither of towpath that once hugged the water to let horses tug boats is now the territory of walkers, cyclists and towpath tourists.

Walkers with cling-wrapped cheese sandwiches, and wide-eyed families with lollipops would have been an unthinkable disturbance along towpaths in the golden era of working canal boats. 'Outsiders' weren't welcome on the towpaths, and blunt signs were erected to damn those who might dare trespass. In an ironic twist of fate, 'keep out' signs have been replaced today with welcoming tourist information boards, and interactive educational signposts. Times have changed, and the message of the signs from two different eras in history must lie back to back in opposition; yet the unifying truth from both messages remains quietly the same - canals are different to the outside world. Whether we're told to keep out, or come in, when we step down onto a towpath we're entering the unique world of canals. A place with its own culture, customs and charms. A destination as different as any faraway place, tantalizingly on Britain's own doorstep.

Towpaths take the willing traveller back to a car-free time where wildlife and nature mingle without the clutter of noise. Nothing hurries, nor moves faster than a duckling trying to keep up with his mum. A priceless treasure trail deliciously scrambles across inland Britain.

WHERE
On canals throughout Britain
The canals are open all day every day - just find your local canal.

MORE INFO
We walk the towpaths from Cornwall up to Scotland - download some of our favourite canal walks. www.coolcanals.com

Visit our website for more about the 100 Treasures, and tell us your favourite treasure www.coolcanals.com/100treasures

RIGHT: Glorious towpath on the Monmouthshire & Brecon Canal
ABOVE: Historic 'keep out' notice (now at the National Waterways Museum) contrasts with the modern message of welcome

86 GLAMORGANSHIRE IRON
Once the most profitable canal in history - a Welsh treasure

> *My favourite treasures - chosen and written by John Bridgeman CBE TD DL:*
> *Vice Chairman of British Waterways and Trustee of the Canal & River Trust.*

" My choice is the remnants of the Glamorganshire Canal and the way it provides echoes and ghosts of the industrial revolution in South Wales all the way up from Cardiff Bay to Merthyr - now in the context of a clean and newly vibrant young society - the real legacy of what was once the most profitable canal in history.

Iron had been produced in Wales in Tudor times but when the Dowlais Ironworks were founded in 1759, Merthyr became for some time the largest centre of iron production in the world. In the early days iron was shipped out by pack horse and mule train but that was terribly limited. Merthyr, the Welsh Valleys and particularly Cardiff were transformed by the construction of the Glamorganshire Canal, 1790-1794, reaching the small town of Cardiff with a population then of less than a thousand.

Admiral Lord Nelson visited Merthyr in 1802 to see cannon being made. They and other iron products were shipped down to Cardiff by 60ft canal boats with a 9ft beam worked by two men and a Welsh pony,

day and night, all year round. Military victories at Trafalgar in 1805 and Waterloo in 1815 were made possible with the help of cannon cast from Welsh iron and shipped out by Welsh canal boatmen.

Until overtaken by the railways, the Glamorganshire Canal was one of the most profitable in history and it laid the platform for that small coast township of Cardiff eventually to become a massive railway terminus, next the world's biggest coal exporter and now the capital of Wales. The canal finally closed for traffic in 1951 but the people of Wales have a new feeling for their heritage ('treftadaeth' in Welsh).

Many remnants of the great Glamorganshire Canal remain, some have been restored, many more wait to be discovered. These remnants and the stories they tell are a real treasure of Britain's historic waterways.

To begin that discovery one must start in Cardiff Bay – a bustling modern waterfront complete with the icons of 21st-century Wales, including the Senedd, home of the Welsh Assembly Government and the much loved Pierhead Building. Built in 1894, the Pierhead Building was once the headquarters of the Port of Cardiff and is now a visitor centre where one can learn something of the history of the Glamorganshire Canal. It's just as it was when the great sea lock of the canal met the tidal waters of the Severn Estuary although nothing remains today of the sea lock or surrounding wharves – all now buried under new streets.

But north of the Great Western Railway line into Cardiff Central Station the echoes become louder and stronger. Original canalside buildings and structures begin to appear, no longer just remnants but part of the Glamorganshire Canal's Heritage. In Mill Lane and the Hayes there are still original 19th-century buildings with listed frontages still as they were in canal times when the canal ran right alongside. Further on, the canal went underground to pass under Queen Street and re-emerge at the foot of the eastern walls of Cardiff Castle. Thereafter the canal followed the route of what is now the long North Road car park with plentiful sightings of the old canal wall before becoming a footpath leading into the Taff Trail. This 55-mile route from Cardiff Bay to Brecon then follows the River Taff before rejoining the line of the Canal at Forest Farm in Whitchurch, the only significant stretch of the canal still in water. At Melingriffith, location of a famous tinplate works, one can now see the fully restored Water Lift Engine – the only one of its kind in the world and re-commissioned in 2011 as a result of efforts by the Oxford House Industrial History Society and the Inland Waterways Association with enlightened financial support from Cardiff City Council and CADW, the official guardian of the built heritage in Wales.

Weighing machines were a rare phenomenon on Britain's canals but one was built for the Glamorganshire at Tongwynlais and later moved to Cardiff. The massive structure could weigh up to 40 tons with an accuracy of 14 pounds by means of a balance leverage of 112:1. It is so valuable historically that it was moved to the Inland Waterways Museum at Stoke Bruerne.

Next on a journey north one can still see the Nantgarw Pottery built alongside the route of the canal – ideal for bringing bulky raw materials in and shipping product out in a necessarily gentle way. For 7 all-to-brief years from 1813, William Billingsley and his son-in-law Samuel Walker made an exquisite soft paste fine porcelain as good as any the world has seen. It is very rare, highly prized amongst collectors but because of the amount of rejected output was never economic. Some of the finest pieces can be found at the National Museum of Wales in Cardiff.

Intrepid explorers will find many charming and hospitable inns and pubs along the route of the old canal – barge work was thirsty work – and especially in old Newbridge, now Pontypridd. Another item of heritage conservation in the making is a new supermarket planned with the intention of sympathetic treatment of another remnant of canal at Ynysyngharad, scene of the world famous Brown Lenox Chainworks. Captain Samuel Brown was a naval officer who saw the advantage of using wrought iron chain instead of hemp rope hawsers on capital ships and after one trial in 1808 the navy immediately ordered 4 warships to be equipped with iron cable. By 1811 chain cables were used on all capital ships and to meet the explosion in demand, Brown and his partner Samuel Lenox built a new factory alongside the canal just outside Newbridge. Iron came down from Merthyr, was forged by blacksmith chain makers and then shipped out from the port of Cardiff. It was a world class business and as well as the Cunarders Aquitania and Mauretania, Brown Lenox anchor chain was used for the QE2. Sadly the chain works are no longer but a small section of canal remains – sensitively restored, it will offer yet another opportunity to celebrate an illustrious past.

North of Pontypridd there is still more to discover – all the way to the restored canal basin at Merthyr. It can be seen on foot, by bicycle or by car with a good map. Signposting is gradually improving. There are tramways and watercourses, canalside cottages and canal company buildings and plenty more inns and pubs on the way. It's all well worth a visit. **"** JOHN BRIDGEMAN

WHERE
Glamorganshire Canal
Cardiff. OS ST192744

MORE INFO
The Pierhead Building in Cardiff is Grade I-listed. www.pierhead.org

Nantgarw Pottery www.nantgarwchinaworksmuseum.co.uk National Museum of Wales www.museumwales.ac.uk

Melingriffith Water Pump is a Scheduled Ancient Monument. www.friendsofmelingriffithwaterpump.org

CADW www.cadw.wales.gov.uk Oxford House Industrial History Society www.riscamuseum.org.uk

Visit our website for more about the 100 Treasures, and tell us your favourite treasure www.coolcanals.com/100treasures

STOKE BRUERNE MUSEUM
A canal village and its museum

The thatched village of Stoke Bruerne and its small museum are inseparable attractions in a canal hub that is full to the brim with living heritage.

Landlubbers and boaters stand around chatting and hives of gongoozlers buzz over the lock to watch narrowboats that pass through the heart of the village. The village is over 1,000 years old, but the canal didn't arrive until 1793. When navvies turned up with their shovels, they hacked the route of the water road, cutting through the village to create the shape of Stoke Bruerne that is much loved today.

Blisworth Tunnel (the third longest on the canal networks) and the Grand Junction Canal were completed in 1805. The tunnel entrance is a short stroll beyond the village hub. As the tunnel doesn't have a towpath and boats had to be legged through, the old stables near the tunnel entrance were once used by boat horses. Diesel engines do the work now, but the visitor who finds a perch near the entrance and peers into the darkness, can imagine the plight of the legger of yore. The Boat Inn, back in the canal village, would have been consolation for the canal worker, and pub goers today can taste the unspoilt charms of this historic building. The Woodward family have been running the pub for 4 generations since 1877, magnificently keeping the home fires burning and the real ales pouring for the canal village.

The museum sits opposite the pub, on the other side of the canal, sharing the same casual arena that says 'pop in'. There's no pomp or starch and the intrigue is instant in the cosy clutter on the ground floor where the museum shop is crammed with souvenirs, books, plum preserve and the essential coasters everyone wants to take home with them as a reminder of a day out. Wooden floorboards thump to the rhythm of the tourist shuffle and a staircase leads from the ground floor to two further levels.

A different mood wafts upstairs, with stone walls and displays that snatch the eye. The canal story is told through films, exhibits of historic tools and clothing, photographs and models. There's a focus on local stories, including the inspiring work of Sister Mary Ward who cared for working boat families in her tiny surgery near Top Lock. She delivered boatwomen's babies and gave families medical treatment for free when they were ill, gaining their trust in an era when the outside world often saw boat families as unsavoury folk.

Stoke Bruerne Museum spreads outside with a

ABOVE: Heading out of the village

historic boat on the canalside and audio trails for little people who like to run around and explore the world of canals in their own excited way. There's a calendar of festivals, events and activities that don't just keep the hub busy, but also help keep waterways heritage alive.

LOCATION

Grand Union Canal
Stoke Bruerne. OS SP743499
Open daily April to October. Winter opening times vary. Small admission charge. Café and gift shop. No wheelchair access to the museum galleries upstairs - there's access to a short film of the collection. Canalside picnic areas outside and audio trail to follow along the towpath. Discount for Friends of the Canal & River Trust.

MORE INFO

Boat Trips
There are boat trips available from outside the museum and the Boat Inn.

www.stokebruerneboats.co.uk www.boatinn.co.uk

Stoke Bruerne Canal Museum is Grade II-listed.

Regular events are held along the canal side including the yearly 'Village At War' when the village takes on a distinctly 1940s feel.

T:01604 862229 www.stokebruernecanalmuseum.org.uk

Visit our website for more about the 100 Treasures, and tell us your favourite treasure www.coolcanals.com/100treasures

Not all treasures of the built canal environment scream from the skies as Pontcysyllte Aqueduct does, or rumble from the bowels of the earth like Standedge Tunnel. The fanfares they blow are real, but along everyone's local canal the tiniest things can reach in gently and mean as much. A small milepost, sitting unceremoniously tucked between weeds along the canal towpath might not make the rank of a mention in many guidebooks - but the passerby who overlooks them, misses the part these posts play in the story of Britain's canals.

Mileposts are stalwart gems of history, scattered at regular intervals along the towpaths. Catch a glimpse of a milepost today and the Industrial Revolution is staring you in the eye. This is hidden history that can be touched and connected with, in the freedom of the fresh air.

Canals were built under Acts of Parliament and mileposts were required to tell working boatmen the distances they had travelled and therefore how much toll would be due to canal companies who charged on a ton and mile basis. During the original working life of the canals, every canal company had its own style of mileposts.

The fascinating story of the milepost doesn't stop with the Victorians. During World War II canal mileposts became a matter of national security and many were removed to prevent Nazi invaders mapping the country. Some of those signs were lost or melted down for the war effort, but many were returned to their rightful place on the canals after the war. Sometimes replica mileposts had to be made, and they were usually slightly altered to avoid confusion with the originals.

Mileposts hold the clues of the past for the canal detective, and are an inspiring example of how the canals of Britain have carved their own story in the living landscape.

WHERE
On canals throughout Britain
The canals are open all day every day - just find your local canal.

MORE INFO
Historic examples of milepost or milestones can be seen at Ellesmere Yard on the Shropshire Union Canal, in the National Waterways Museum at Ellesmere Port, and in other waterways museums such as Gloucester and Stoke Bruerne.

www.nwm.org.uk   www.gloucesterwaterwaysmuseum.org.uk   www.stokebruernecanalmuseum.org.uk

The Milestone Society's aim is to 'identify, record, research, conserve and interpret for public benefit the milestones and other waymarkers of the British Isles'. Their website includes a database of almost all visible milestones in Britain.

www.milestonesociety.co.uk

Visit our website for more about the 100 Treasures, and tell us your favourite treasure www.coolcanals.com/100treasures

ABOVE: Grade II-listed cast-iron milepost at Shardlow on the Trent & Mersey Canal
RIGHT: This milestone near bridge 33 on the Macclesfield Canal is also Grade II-listed

Fire-spitting chimneys once choked the landscape across the north of England, and the area still harbours secrets from the heyday of those dark Satanic Mills. Preserved buildings can hold an aura of iconic loneliness in the memory of textile workers who endured poverty, disease and overcrowded housing. But Sir Titus Salt's mill is a breath of fresh air, standing boldly by the Leeds & Liverpool Canal and the River Aire. His mill's redundant chimney looms down from the sky like a public monument with a silent story that wants to be heard.

Sir Titus Salt (1803-1876) built an entire village for his mill workers. Neat rows of terraced houses line 22 streets, there's a school, a hospital, two churches and a workers' institute. The village of Saltaire is a testament to the philanthropic ideals Salt, and some of the most successful entrepreneurs of the canal era, passionately adhered to. Many Quakers such as the Cadbury family and other non-conformist church reformers such as Titus Salt proved by example that success in business could be built on fair trade. Saltaire was a place where weavers earned a modest wage working for the textile industry that dominated world markets. Unlike some less ethical mill owners, Salt cared that his workers were able to maintain a certain standard of living, and so he provided his workers with a well-built home in his village.

The Industrial Revolution was bringing radical change, with migration of the work force to new industries along the canals, and the new pecking order of social classes riled in rabid confusion. The houses in Saltaire must have seemed superior to houses other mill workers lived in, with reliable patterns of windows and doors offering security and comfort in a time of chaos. Salt aimed to nurture a community with one common cause - the mill.

The cobbled streets are still alive today, in a real village with private residents and tourists who tiptoe around. The village is a thriving example of living heritage, immaculately preserved with ordinary daily life carrying on. Little has changed on the surface, except the armies of wheelie bins that line the back alleyways for a throwaway culture that Saltaire's original villagers wouldn't have understood.

The mill has been converted into an art and shopping experience. It houses the largest permanent collection of David Hockney paintings and on separate floors there are books, jewellery and other temptations. The huge mill still echoes with the acoustics of a cathedral of the manufacturing industry, except that the bellow of looms has been replaced by background recordings of classical music. Bare bricks arch overhead and stone floors hold feet firm, leaving the imagination to picture the mill as it was. The stairs that lead through the levels are away from the fuss and, in their emptiness, they perhaps hold the real spirit of the people who once trudged up and down them in a day's work.

Salt's mill once housed 1,200 looms producing 30,000 yards of alpaca and other cloths every day. Steam-driven machinery needed 50 tons of coal per day and water was drawn from the River Aire through pipes that ran under the building and the canal.

Exploring the whole village today is a social, political and industrial commentary, but the odd thing about Saltaire is how soothing its 'order' is. The best way to end a good day out is with a pint of ale, and in Saltaire it's an irreverent must. In his mission to provide good welfare for his workers, Titus Salt insisted that no pub should be allowed in his village. Over a hundred years after his death the Boathouse Inn was opened right next to his mill. A second pub then had the audacity to open in the tree-lined main street in the village. It is cheekily called 'Don't Tell Titus'. Who would dare.

WHERE

Huddersfield Narrow Canal

Saltaire OS SE139381

The village of Saltaire is like any other - just walk its streets and use its shops and cafés. Salts Mill is open daily. Shops, cafés and exhibitions. FREE admission.

MORE INFO

The entire Victorian industrial village of Saltaire is a designated UNESCO World Heritage Site. whc.unesco.org/en/list

For more about Titus Salt, his vision, his mill and the village of Saltaire. www.saltairevillage.info

Saltaire Visitor Information Centre is inside Salts Mill.

T:01274 437942 www.visitbradford.com

T:01274 531163 www.saltsmill.org.uk

Visit our website for more about the 100 Treasures, and tell us your favourite treasure www.coolcanals.com/100treasures

HOTEL BOAT
Tradition meets tourism

Freshly baked cakes, afternoon tea and a pre-dinner drink in the lounge before a feast, then off to bed to be lulled to sleep by the sounds of silence over the water. A floating hotel has obvious attraction for the holidaymaker, but the business of taking passengers on a cruise along Britain's canals and rivers serves more than one function. Hotel boats not only play a vital role in the leisure industry, which in turn helps Britain's inland waterways to stay viable and vibrant, but many also help to keep canal heritage alive as they are operated using traditional boating skills. When a towpath tourist meets a hotel boat, serious bouts of waving and nodding are guaranteed.

Hotel boats range from boutique style with full frills and Jacuzzi, to 5-star traditional comforts, and even to the budget muck-in floating dorm. Some hotel boats are converted historic boats, others are newly built with bespoke fittings. Many are narrowboats that quietly explore the rolling landscapes in greenest England and a few are bigger boats that stride into the feisty waters of the Scottish Highlands. But every hotel boat that travels the inland waterways shares one aim, which is to pamper its guests. "Wonderful" was the single word passengers aboard Bywater Hotel Boat Cruises used unanimously to describe their 2012 summer holiday on the water.

ABOVE: Bywater's 'Kerala' towing butty boat 'Karnataka'

Every narrowboat that travels the waterways is a floating 'Tardis' with miraculous facilities that unfold and swivel from any corner and crevice. There are usually cabins to sleep in with mini ensuite, a lounge, a sociable dining area for traditional canal chatter, and decks for lazy daylong cruise-snoozing. Passengers choose whether to walk on ahead to be alone, or help at the locks or do absolutely nothing! In their holiday literature, Canal Voyagers mention the core basics anyone would need to know before booking a holiday - such as details on cruising itinerary, on-board facilities, meals... and even 'elevenses'. But there's a hunch between the lines that elevenses can be any time of day by 'canal-time' on a hotel boat holiday.

Several companies such as Bywater, Duke & Duchess and Canal Voyagers have two narrowboats that work as a pair in the traditional working boat style - with a powered boat that tows an unpowered boat, called a butty. The crew has to navigate the same tight bridges, impossible Brindley bends and torturous lock flights as a working boat would have done over 200 years ago. The towing rope, the barge pole and the boatman's kettle all milk their worth, and teamwork is demonstratively visible. There is something about a pair of narrowboats on the move

that is deeply satisfying to watch. The tillersman, or tillerswoman, always appears graceful in a stance that fits beautifully into history, and the onlooker's pleasure is to witness the glorious vision of two boats being steered with effortless control. Yet appearances might deceive, since running a hotel boat is never effortless. For the crew, the dawn to dusk job of looking after their boats and passengers has to be more than a job - it's not even a vocation, it's got to be a way of life they just love.

Is there a downside for passengers on hotel boat holidays? The Bywater passengers pause, in a stutter of silence, then with a glint in their eyes they agree, "the cost!" The glint is the secret code that means it is worth every penny. People travel from America, Germany, Scandinavia, South Africa, New Zealand and anywhere in between to experience a holiday on a hotel boat cruising Britain's canals. So, Britain's canals can wave their flags in the global market of tourism, just as they once did in the era of great manufacturing industries.

WHERE
On canals throughout Britain
There are hotel boats ranging from traditional narrowboat pairs cruising the historic waterways of England, to huge converted barges in the Highlands of Scotland. The canals are open all day every day - just find your local canal and you may be lucky enough to spot a hotel boat on the move.

MORE INFO
Full listings of all hotel boats in Britain can be found in our online directory.

www.coolcanals.com

Visit our website for more about the 100 Treasures, and tell us your favourite treasure www.coolcanals.com/100treasures

When the bunting comes out, everyone knows the canals are about to party! No well-organised national canal festival or humble local gathering would be complete without a jolly draping of bunting.

Every year the big event that unravels yards of flags is Crick Boat Show. The marina at Crick, on the grand Union Canal in Northamptonshire bursts at the seams with hundreds of gleaming boats, all butting side by side. Crick Show is the chance for festival goers to nose through dizzy numbers of spanking new boats and dream of buying (or buy!). When the sun shines, fresh strawberries are served and folk stretch out on the sun-toasted grass, and when it rains everyone talks about the weather as wellies wade through mud. But rain or shine, the boot-stomping music plays on, and the beer tent rocks with the famous canal camaraderie.

ABOVE: Hanging out the bunting at a boat festival

Around the last weekend in June bunting is in demand across the country as festival fever steams ahead. Braunston Historic Boat Rally is a thrilling event that seems to attract more boats and people than any tiny water village should. Restored, preserved, adored and adorned narrowboats arrive by water road from all corners of the country to congregate at the rally. Old friends and old boats gather with blatant glee, and the party atmosphere nonchalantly carries a floating display of nationally important living heritage. This event is a parade for pleasure with the biggest gathering of museum worthy boats. The bunting flaps in a flurry over gasping crowds as 70ft narrowboats dance together and tillersmen smile from ear to ear. Wherever there's a boat festival, the aromas of sun cream and oily rags waft together over the sounds of Morris men jiggling and the rhythmic baritone putt-putt-put-putt of a historic narrowboat engine. Who says history is boring? The boats and the bunting keep living history in canal style.

London has its own bunting for Little Venice, the sleepiest corner of the city, when the Cavalcade puts on its colourful event every May bank holiday. And Canal Street in Manchester's gay village abandons all inhibition, screaming with tiaras and rainbow bunting for the annual Pride event every year. Almost every city and county in the nation has a reason to party along its canal at some time in the year.

Even the word 'bunting' is pleasing to say aloud, with Pavlovian stocks of happy days out as a child. The origins of the word aren't known, but there are plenty of fascinating facts that can lead to guesses (even with the canals involved by proxy). The textile industry of the late 17th century created a lightweight worsted wool fabric called bunting. And as language evolves, words from the textile industry have new meanings that derive from previous function (such as cheese cloth). 'Baby bunting' was a loose cloth that babies were wrapped in and bunting was also the perfect cloth to make flags and ribbons - which were items of everyday working life for traditional boat families of that time. The cloth is also linked with naval ships. Historically, flags were used as a way for ships to signal to others, and the signalman who prepared and flew the flag

hoists was called the 'bunting tosser'. Naval slang today still calls its signalman 'bunts' even though the role has changed unrecognisably.

Just as bunting was a boatman's signal, when lines of tidy plastic bunting wave across the inland waterways, they are really just signalling 'come to a party!'

At any time of year, at any place across over 2,000 miles of inland waterways, there's always a sleepy narrowboat with a faded old bundle of knotted bunting just waiting for the call to be reeled out. Bunting means something to people and every part of the process, from untangling last year's mayhem from the store box, then deciding the best angle to drape the line, and who will help on the ladder, is part of the special experience. Putting up bunting isn't a solo task, it's a preparation for a party, holding the hope of people's elation in every fibre.

So bunting is a tradition steeped in history, and has to be a treasure of the canals because it is the symbol of something happening that is fun to share, and that's a sentiment close to the heart of canal culture.

WHERE
On canals throughout Britain
The canals are open all day every day - just find your local canal. Bunting of course takes centre stage at waterways festivals and events throughout the year.

MORE INFO
Full listings of festivals and events on Britain's canals can be found in our online directory.

www.coolcanals.com

Visit our website for more about the 100 Treasures, and tell us your favourite treasure www.coolcanals.com/100treasures

92 RAYMOND
Britain's last unpowered wooden commercial narrowboat

Some historic boats ooze instant appeal and draw dilated eyes and tender caresses wherever they travel along the canals. Raymond is the last unpowered wooden narrowboat built to carry commercial cargo in Britain, and there can be few boats that capture the adoration of so many. Raymond is beautiful, but good looks are not all this boat has to be proud of. When a restored and preserved historic boat is lovingly paraded anywhere on the inland waterways today, there's usually a life story behind the bright colours and polished brass that commands the very best salute.

Raymond was built for Samuel Barlow Coal Carrying Company in 1958. Without an engine, Raymond worked as a pair, in tow with another motorised boat. Narrowboat Nutfield was Raymond's long-time companion carrying coal from the Midlands to London. Raymond was a regular on the notorious Jam 'Ole run on the Paddington Arm of the Grand Union. Here imported fruit pulp arrived from London Docks for the jam factory. The Jam 'Ole got its name from the boat crews that navigated their way into the dock that served the factory. It had to be accessed through a bridge, and since working boaters called all bridges 'bridge oles', the obvious happened.

From 1962 to 1970 Blue Line Canal Carriers Ltd operated the boat and during its working lifetime Raymond was operated by Arthur and Rose Bray. Being their home as well as a working boat, when trade ceased in 1970 the Brays still lived aboard until 1980, when Jim and Doris Collins bought the boat and they moved in to live aboard until 1993.

There were plans to restore the boat after that, but Raymond was too tired to wait and sadly sank. The charisma of this vessel called out and in 1996 the Friends of Raymond formed to save the vessel. Raymond was refloated and towed to the Black Country Living Museum. But before restoration could begin, the dilapidated boat sank again. As much as could be salvaged was used in the valiant restoration project that followed and on 3 July 2000, Raymond was returned to Braunston Marina near the place where the boat had been first built over 42 years prior.

Raymond's boatman's cabin was restored with traditional lacework and lace plates and all the glorious functional fittings Arthur and Rose Bray would have needed to make Raymond their home. This boat has become a living document of historical importance. And like the best Mills and Boon tearjerker, Nutfield and Raymond were eventually reunited at their water base in Braunston.

WHERE
Raymond can be seen at Braunston Marina, Grand Union Canal, or at waterways festivals and events throughout the year. There is always an opportunity to see Raymond and Nutfield, and ask the crew members more about the boats.

MORE INFO
For Raymond's full itinerary, visit their website. Raymond is looked after by volunteers, the Friends of Raymond, who are always looking for new members and trainees to learn how to operate the two boats.

Raymond is listed on the National Register of Historic Vessels (NRHV). www.nationalhistoricships.org.uk

Friends of Raymond www.thefriendsofraymond.org.uk

Visit our website for more about the 100 Treasures, and tell us your favourite treasure www.coolcanals.com/100treasures

RIGHT: Raymond being towed by Nutfield through bridge 1 of the Grand Union Canal at Braunston during the annual Historic Narrowboat Rally

My favourite treasures - chosen and written by Nigel Crowe:
Head of Heritage for the Canal & River Trust

" **According to John Betjeman the Great Western Railway was 'the greatest railway in the world'.**

Its formations were magnificent and its original, heroic broad gauge (7ft 0 ¼ ins; extraordinary dimensions!) gave all its equipment a giant quality.

From the 1840s onwards the GWR grew powerful, swallowing rival railway companies and absorbing canals in the Midlands and Southwest into its empire. They include the Bridgwater & Taunton, Swansea, Monmouthshire & Brecon, Kennet & Avon and South Stratford Canals.

The canals which fell under its sway still bear the hallmarks of GWR ownership in the form of boundary markers, platelayers' huts, iron fence posts, cross-hatched paving bricks and loading signs. And in the Waterways Archive, there are hundreds of engineering drawings stamped in red ink with the words 'GWR Paddington Station, London'.

The most common GWR relics on canals are Brunel's ill-fated broad gauge 'bridge' rails. In the 1890s the broad gauge was abandoned. Its locomotives and rolling stock were scrapped at Swindon and its bridge rails were chopped up and recycled for use on canals as stanchions for signs, mile plates and roller winches. Scattered along towpaths and hedgerows, these rusty rails are poignant reminders of the giant steam trains which once thundered along Brunel's permanent way to the West of England. Examples of GWR memorabilia abound on the Kennet & Avon Canal, especially its Wiltshire sections. "
NIGEL CROWE

WHERE
On canals throughout Britain
The canals are open all day every day - just find your local canal.

MORE INFO
The Museum of the Great Western Railway is based in Swindon, the former heart of the GWR rail network.

www.steam-museum.org.uk

Engineering drawings and other GWR artefacts can be seen in the National Waterways Archive, based at the National Waterways Museum. The Archive can be visited by appointment and can also be searched online.

www.nwm.org.uk

Visit our website for more about the 100 Treasures, and tell us your favourite treasure www.coolcanals.com/100treasures

RIGHT: In competition with each other from the start, and inseparable still, railways and canals have scratched the landscape together and shared history across every corner of Britain - as here at Consall Forge on the Caldon Canal

94 STOURPORT BASINS
A unique canal town

Stourport-on-Severn is the only town in Britain that was built solely for the canals. It has evolved into a unique place today, with a distinct travelling ethos.

The town was born out of James Brindley's fantastical idea of creating a 'Grand Cross' through a network of canals that would link the rivers Mersey, Trent, Severn and Thames. The River Severn was England's busiest river, transporting cargo from Bristol to the Midlands. Its furthest navigable point was Bewdley, where goods had to be unloaded from boats onto tiny horse-pulled carts that clumsily clopped to land-locked destinations beyond. The Industrial Revolution's lust for speed was champing for Brindley's plan.

Following permissions granted in the Parliamentary Act of 1766, Brindley started building the Staffordshire & Worcestershire Canal to link the River Severn to the Trent. But Brindley didn't choose Bewdley to be his port from the River Severn. To keep construction costs tight, he cunningly hitchhiked the less hilly route where the River Stour had already carved its way into the Severn. The nearby hamlet of Lower Mitton was destined to be swamped by the new canal development and the pitiless growth of an important and affluent canal town. Stourport became the busiest inland port in the Midlands after Birmingham.

To allow river boats to turn off the Severn and then load and unload their cargoes onto canal boats, Brindley built a series of locks and basins. The upper and lower basins were linked by a wide barge lock (gobbling 95,000 gallons of water each time it's used) and another barge lock met the Severn. As trade increased, more basins were added, along with two sets of two-rise staircase locks. At Stourport's peak of activity, there were five basins in operation, with warehouses and homes for the workers built around the basins. By 1795 around 1,300 people lived in the town. A ferocious hub of development spread with brass and iron foundries, vinegar works, tan yards, worsted spinning mills, carpet manufacturers, boat building yards, wharfs, shops and inns.

At the same time as building the canal, in 1773 an inn was conveniently positioned on the waterside at the basins. The inn became the Tontine Hotel, used by the canal company as its unofficial business centre. In its grandeur, it offered merchants, high-class employees and passengers plush accommodation and entertainment, including a ballroom and all the fine trimmings of pomposity, all safely away from the haulage trade's swearing boats and uncouth everyday business.

The Tontine is still impressive today, but it is the late 18th-century Clock Warehouse that elegantly dominates the basins. The original warehouse didn't have a clock, and the clock (made by Samuel Thorpe of Abberley) that chimes ceremoniously on the hour, every hour, today was only added by public subscription in 1812. Time has watched over the basins for two centuries, and no tourist who arrives with a camera leaves without a photo of the Clock Warehouse.

Brindley's basins have survived the ups and downs of the canal's fortunes and in 2006 the Heritage Lottery Fund, along with British Waterways (now the Canal & River Trust) & other funders, facilitated the recent restoration of the basins. But not everything has survived the dynamics of change. The old Engine House has gone and instead, a retro fairground squeals with joy on the site that once laboured to hurl water from the river to feed the basins. Boulton & Watt's steam engine was the old beating heart of the basins - tackling 100,000 gallons of water that were lost from the basins every time a canal boat moved to or from the river. Sadly, this masterpiece of engineering was a victim of World War I when it was removed for scrap iron.

The traffic of the Industrial Revolution has gone but, in this millennium, Stourport sits on one of the busiest cruising rings in Britain (aptly known as the Stourport Ring) and holiday boats keep the basins alive. The basins are home to around 100 narrowboats and yachts, and Stourport is famed for prolific gongoozling. A boater's journey from the river twists through impossibly angled basins, forcing formidable manoeuvres under the gauntlet of gongoozlers.

Stourport-on-Severn is a Georgian town with a population of around 20,000 people, but it is bulked by the hordes who pilgrim here every summer to eat fish and chips, stroll along the river banks, shriek down the helter-skelter and endlessly gongoozle. The town's adjacent shopping street and the basins don't easily tally together, and we have a hunch that if Mr Brindley could have his say, he'd claim the real treasure of Stourport still lies firmly in its water.

LOCATION

Staffordshire & Worcestershire Canal
Stourport-on-Severn. OS SO810710
Stourport Basins are where the Staffordshire & Worcestershire Canal meets the river Severn. The Basins are open all day every day. FREE admission.

MORE INFO

Stourport Basins, locks and wharfs, and many of the cottages are Grade II-listed. The former stables for the Tontine Hotel (now private apartments) are also Grade II-listed, and now house the Tontine Stable Heritage Room where you can pick up the Discovery Trail leaflet and find out more about the Basins. Follow the Discovery Trail to find out more about the Basins, their heritage and their regeneration. The Basins have also been awarded the Transport Trust Red Wheel Plaque.

www.transporttrust.com   www.transportheritage.com

ww.stourporttown.co.uk

Visit our website for more about the 100 Treasures, and tell us your favourite treasure www.coolcanals.com/100treasures

Historic warehouses, aqueducts, tunnels, lock flights - canal history shouts across the landscape with the voice of the built environment telling the world about those great engineers and entrepreneurs who built the canals. But behind the dazzle of that limelight, there's a different tiny space that holds the humble story of the ordinary champions of the canals. Working boat crews lived aboard their craft in a cramped 10ft space at the stern, known as the boatman's cabin. The original boatman's cabins of historic boats are the storytellers of an intimate and discreet treasure.

ABOVE: The kettle takes pride of place inside historic working boat 'Northwich', Gloucester Waterways Museum

The boatman's cabin has become the romantic symbol of hardship and pride that defines the families who crewed canal boats. And when the opportunity to explore inside a historic boat lets you clamber into the cooped den that was once home to a family, the reality of 10ft by 7ft reaches deeper than a romantic cliché.

By modern standards, with king-size everything and walk-in fridges, the size of a boat-home is shocking, but working boat families had an outdoor lifestyle and the cabin served as a practical place for cooking, sleeping and shelter. Hardships had to be cushioned by the strength of the canal community.

Canal boat folk were seen as a different 'race' by those who lived on land, and were often treated with suspicion or fear. In their segregation from mainstream society, they had their own culture and traditions that in turn kept the 'races' apart and prejudices were a constant challenge.

In the early years of Canal Mania, it was only men who worked on the boats, but when competition from the railways forced the economic slump on the canal, the boatmen had to give up their houses and bring their families to live afloat and help crew the boat. Every member of the family had their role. Most of the children were illiterate, with no time for school as they were in charge of daily jobs such as walking with the horse or operating the locks. The men often squeezed in time to supplement food supplies by poaching rabbits, fishing for eels or pulling vegetables from fields along the canal side. And the women worked robust hours on the tiller as well as cooking and cleaning.

Every crevice of the boatman's cabin was used ingeniously to create a cosy and functional home for the whole family. Cupboards open and become table surfaces, a bed folds out from a 'bunkhole' that is a place to sit in the daytime. A coal-fired range is the heart of the cabin as it heats the boat, cooks the food and dries the washing too. Brass and lace were a matter of pride and traditional canal painting decorated every surface available.

ABOVE: Historic photograph of a boat family christening at Long Buckby on the Grand Union Canal
(National Waterways Archive)

Some of the best preserved examples of a boatman's cabin invite visitors to crouch inside the dark space and mind they don't bump into now idle pots and pans hanging overhead. The space carries powerful memories of the people whose labour served a nation that wanted to build its empire. Any quiet moment inside a real boatman's cabin is a privilege that sparks the imagination in the presence of historic domestic paraphernalia. In the corner where the stove sits, a statuesque kettle on the stove might sing silently in remembrance of the colourful folk that once danced, played and worked on the canals.

WHERE
Inside traditional narrowboats on canals throughout Britain.
There are opportunities to climb into traditional boats and experience the reality of a boatman's cabin at the National Waterways Museum at Ellesmere Port, and other waterways museums such as Gloucester, London and Stoke Bruerne.

www.nwm.org.uk   www.gloucesterwaterwaysmuseum.org.uk   www.stokebruernecanalmuseum.org.uk

MORE INFO
Historic boats travel around the networks to attend canal festivals and boat gatherings, such as the Braunston Historic Narrowboat Rally on the Grand Union Canal, offering more chances to see the tiny space which is the boatman's cabin.

www.braunstonmarina.co.uk   www.hnbc.org.uk

Visit our website for more about the 100 Treasures, and tell us your favourite treasure www.coolcanals.com/100treasures

96 LLANGOLLEN WHARF
Historic hoof prints meet tourist footprints

Sheep, green fields and flags of red dragons wave over Llangollen. This part of Denbighshire screams with Welsh charm that butts farmers and tourists together - and the canal joins in with its own special attraction. Llangollen Wharf sits high above town, overlooking its territory as if time has halted since the canal was first built.

Llangollen is most famous for being the festival capital of Wales, and the world turns up on its doorstep every year for the International Music Eisteddfod. This historic town also brings visitors to a Celtic castle, Castell Dinas Bran, that was left in ruins on top of a mountain looming over the canal from afar; then there's Valle Crucis Abbey where Cistercian monks once wandered around; and there's a railway that operates steam and heritage diesel trains. All year round, there's enough sightseeing to keep everyone busy, but Llangollen Wharf is the best place to explore the town's glamorous waterways heritage.

The Llangollen Canal is one of Britain's most popular canals, and narrowboats clutter the route as far as they can go. The wharf is a busy little hub where landlubbing tourists mingle with those who queue to board the trip boat that takes passengers to the very end of Llangollen's waterways trail. There's a tearoom for hungry visitors to tuck into Bara Brith (Welsh cake), and then pop into the shop next door to buy a souvenir to take home. Old and young, and all ages between, wait for their turn on the horse-drawn trip boat. A romantic aroma kicks wafts of dust in time with hoof prints as magnificent horses plod along the towpath, towing their narrowboat full of passengers. This is a trip boat that carries on its peaceful way as if man had never invented the noisy engine, and passengers are clearly delighted to place their trust in the power of a gentle giant instead.

Horseshoe Falls is at the end of the Llangollen Canal, just a short way from the wharf. This impressive semi-circular weir across the River Dee is Telford's dramatic finale for Llangollen's waterway. But the crashing water from the weir is not just for effect, it keeps a constant supply of water flowing into the canal - an amazing 12 million gallons of water flow beyond Llangollen, all the way to Hurleston Reservoir at the other end of the canal. Drama and function are the signature of the Llangollen Canal with Horseshoe Falls, Pontcysyllte Aqueduct, Chirk Aqueduct all doing their best to thrill the traveller and complete a working route too. And at Llangollen Wharf the canal is lightly sprinkled with that irresistibly sweet spice of Welsh tourism that manages to burst with nostalgia and soft adventure at the same time.

WHERE
Llangollen Canal
Llangollen. OS SJ215422
The Wharf is on the hillside overlooking Llangollen, and has a tearoom and gift shop.

MORE INFO
Boat trips
From Llangollen Wharf you can take a horsedrawn boat trip to the end of the canal at Horseshoe Falls or a longer trip along the canal to cross the Pontcysyllte Aqueduct.

T:01978 860702 www.horsedrawnboats.co.uk

11 miles of the Llangollen Canal including Horseshoe Falls, Llangollen Wharf and the Pontcysyllte Aqueduct are designated as a UNESCO World Heritage Site.

www.pontcysyllte-aqueduct.co.uk

Visit our website for more about the 100 Treasures, and tell us your favourite treasure www.coolcanals.com/100treasures

RIGHT: Llangollen Wharf in its mountainous setting

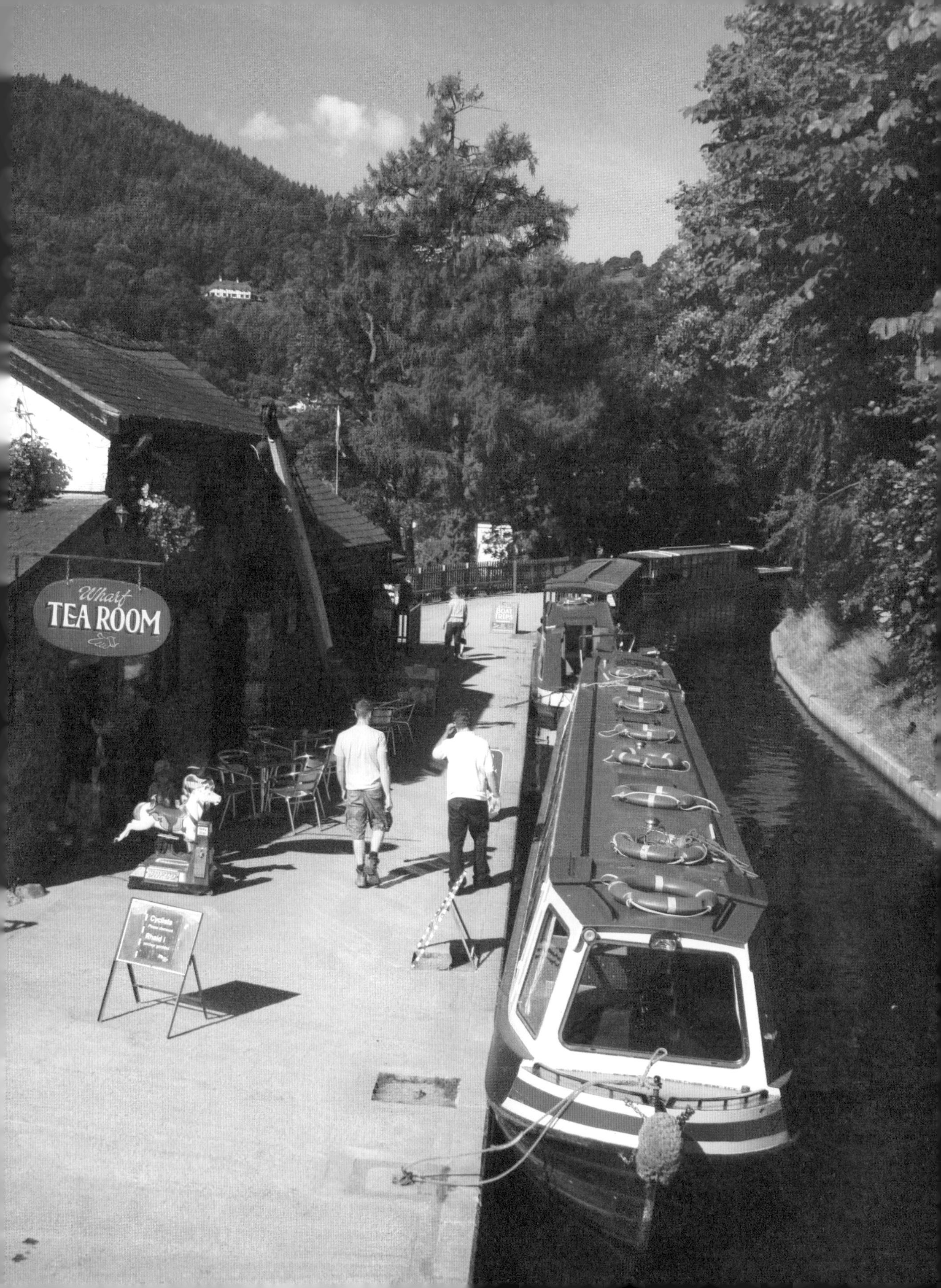
Wharf
TEA ROOM
Cyclists
Rhaid i

A flight of locks rides away from Marple Junction where the Macclesfield and Peak Forest Canals meet. The locks are Grade I-listed and are among the deepest in the country, raising or lowering the Peak Forest Canal 13ft in each step. A climb through the lock flight, whether by boat or on foot, is a goose-bump encounter with history, on a living canal.

The Peak Forest Canal was completed in 1800, but Marple Locks weren't built until 1804. A temporary tramway was used to bridge the one-mile gap until the canal company had enough money to build the flight of locks.

ABOVE: Boat crossing Marple Aqueduct with railway viaduct above

Today, black and white sweeping lock arms dominate the eye, but the Marple lock flight is defined by its delicious stonework. The locks melt into a Peak Forest landscape, jangling with contented nods from walkers and boaters; and the route is an outdoor adventure with the added intrigue of manmade mysteries from the past.

Under the thunder of cascading water falling from one lock chamber to the next, the towpath conceals a secret passageway where the ghosts of working boat horses bawl in rhythm with the water. A tiny arched tunnel, cobbled underfoot, would once have rung with heavy hooves of horses towing canal boats laden with coal and limestone. The tunnel acts as a museum piece, unbothered by labels and barriers as it brazenly stands still for anyone with the will to pass through.

Then the thrill of an even tinier tunnel waits for the explorer - a short, dark, spiralling passageway leads from windswept open views of the canalside to the bottom of the great lock gates where canal water crashes in descent. There's only room for one person at a time in this secret passageway, and the solitude can run riot with the imagination, picturing those who trod here before. This smaller passageway was once used by the crews of traditional working boats and the sensory explosion for today's visitor is to ponder that this journey was just all in a day's work for boating people 200 years ago.

ABOVE: A wooded oasis near the bottom of the lock flight

WHERE

Peak Forest Canal
Marple. OS SE107399

MORE INFO

The walk down the flight is a mix of stonework, black and white lock arms and the greenery from surrounding woodland. A few hundred yards beyond the last lock is the 300ft-long Marple Aqueduct, 100ft above the river Goyt below, with a dramatic railway viaduct towering even higher over it.

Each of the individual locks in the Marple flight and their adjacent footbridges are Grade II-listed, and Marple Aqueduct is a Scheduled Ancient Monument.

Possett Bridge by lock 13 acquired its name because Samuel Oldknow, a local industrialist and promoter of the canal, was anxious that the canal should be finished on time. To spur on the workmen, he had 'ale possets' (hot milk, ale, bread & spice) made for their breakfast by the Navigation Inn nearby. His plan must have worked - the canal was completed in time for Oldknow's boat to make the first trip.

Take a virtual tour of the lock flight with information about the points of interest along the way.

www.marple-uk.com

Visit our website for more about the 100 Treasures, and tell us your favourite treasure www.coolcanals.com/100treasures

My favourite treasures - chosen and written by Nigel Crowe:
Head of Heritage for the Canal & River Trust

❝ Cottages are part of the historic infrastructure of canals.

Most of them were built between the 1790s and the 1930s to house lockkeepers, bridge-keepers, toll clerks and other canal company staff.

ABOVE: Overlooking Neptune's Staircase on the Caledonian Canal, this listed former lockkeeper's cottage built by Thomas Telford is now available for holiday lets through the Vivat Trust

In the 1950s and 1960s the number of canal cottages declined. Remote examples without sanitation or electricity were especially vulnerable. Withdrawal of staff often led to neglect and demolition. More recently the value - in financial and historic terms - of canal cottages has been recognised and the best examples are now listed or lie within conservation areas.

In the past few years the Canal & River Trust has carefully refurbished a number of cottages and found beneficial new uses for them. The stone-built Salterhebble Lock cottage on the Calder & Hebble and the white-rendered cottage at Stocker's Lock on the Grand Union are examples of successful refurbishment schemes - the latter forms part of a classic set-piece ensemble of lock, bridge (with wartime relics), larger canal house and coal duty boundary marker. **❞**
NIGEL CROWE

WHERE
On canals throughout Britain
The canals are open all day every day - just find your local canal.

MORE INFO
Some lock cottages are now available for holiday let. Full listings of holiday cottages on Britain's canals can be found in our online directory.

www.coolcanals.com

Landmark Trust www.landmarktrust.org.uk

Vivat Trust www.vivat-trust.org

Visit our website for more about the 100 Treasures, and tell us your favourite treasure www.coolcanals.com/100treasures

RIGHT: The Landmark Trust look after historic properties for holiday let such as this former lockkeeper's cottage on the Tardebigge Flight of the Worcester & Birmingham Canal

Stourbridge doesn't pretend to be a tourist beauty spot, but its skyline peaks with pride over the Red House Glass Cone, and tourists come in their hoards. Stourbridge was once world renowned for its glassmaking, and the Red House Glass Cone pierces the sky with the audacity of a cathedral of the glass industry. There are only four glass cones left standing in Britain, and Stourbridge can claim the best preserved across Europe. The Cone is a tourist attraction that is a deep-reaching experience.

When Red House Glass Cone was built at the end of the 18th century, it stood in a landscape riddled with cones that huffed and puffed together. Now, the lone survivor stacks 200 years of history in the intensely beautiful spiral pattern of its bricks.

The most recent glass production was by Stuart Crystal who produced glass inside the cone until 1936, then in a factory on the site, until production stopped in 2001. In March 2002 the cone opened as a museum.

From outside, the cone is powerful, striking and still, but the hollow space inside belts the visitor with the spirit of the burning flames of its past. Spreading 60ft wide and reaching 100ft high, it was built by Richard Bradley in 1788 - 1794, and its unaltered structure leaves authenticity for the imagination. From the dark sweaty centre of the cone, the eye is torn upwards by concentric circles of bricks reaching to the dot of light at the top. The cone shape drew air into the furnace to make the fire burn hotter, and here the glass worker earned his living through the flames of an unholy heat. The ferocity of the furnace that once bellowed from the spot shivers through the feet of visitors who take turn to stand here in silent remembrance.

The visitors' centre holds displays of historic tools, has self-guided audio tours and offers regular glassblowing demonstrations. In contrast to the industrial darkness and heat inside the Cone, the adjacent shop sparkles delicately with light from rows of shelves stacked with fine glass artefacts.

The glass industry used the canal to transport its wares and Red House Glass Cone sits conveniently on the Stourbridge Canal, by Glassworks Bridge on the Stourbridge Sixteen Locks. The museum has a canalside tearoom evocatively on the spot where narrowboats once loaded cargo from the Cone - the 21st-century intrusion is sensitive, and forgiven as it adds the obligatory cuppa, or more, for an utterly satisfying day out.

WHERE
Stourbridge Canal
Stourbridge. OS SO894864
Open daily all year. FREE admission. Galleries, gift shop and tearoom. Audio guide. Regular exhibitions, events, workshops and glassblowing demonstrations.

MORE INFO
Red House Glass Cone is Grade II*-listed.

The Cone plays a pivotal role in the International Festival of Glass which takes place every other year in the Stourbridge Glass Quarter. One of the highlights of the Festival is the British Glass Biennale which is a major exhibition of British contemporary glass.

www.ifg.org.uk

T:01384 812750 www.redhousecone.co.uk

RIGHT: Red House Glass Cone on the Stourbridge Canal

In 2012, with the launch of the new charity 'Canal & River Trust', a new logo was needed to represent the changes for Britain's inland waterways. Over 2,000 miles of canals and rivers are now in the care of the charity, and as a momentous fresh era dawns, the powerfully simple image of a swan afloat under a bridge carries the message of the waterways. The logo of the Canal & River Trust is an iconic symbol for the canals of our time.

John Rushworth, partner at Pentagram design agency, was behind the previous British Waterways logo designed in the 1980s, and the Waterways Trust logo. When the inland waterways were about to transfer to charity status, he volunteered his time for free to help create the new Canal & River Trust logo. The swan won the star role in his design.

"The swan is probably the most iconic bird in Britain and it's what you see, and more importantly notice, when you visit the canal. The swan also encompasses many of the traits the Canal & River Trust will need to possess. It's nurturing, yet protective and ready to defend its territory."
John Rushworth.

The canals are manmade, yet live entwined with nature, and the logo is the face of that seamless union. The still silence of this graphic flags the fabulously diverse voice of Britain's canals and rivers. It melts the past, present and future in a visual meeting place packed with the emotion that connects everyone who visits.

Just as its predecessor, the British Waterways logo did, the Canal & River Trust's logo stamps the romantic black and white colours synonymous with the canals. Wherever it appears across the built environment of the canals of Britain - on lock arms, on plaques and signposts, over bridges and inside tunnels, dotted over cobblestoned corners and windswept towpaths - it becomes part of the waterways landscape itself. In a touching twist, it is much more than just a logo, it becomes part of the environment it represents.

WHERE
Throughout England & Wales
The canals are open all day every day - just find your local canal.

MORE INFO
Canal & River Trust/Glandwr Cymru is responsible for over 2,200 miles of canals and rivers in England & Wales. The Canal & River Trust's official leisure guide to canals, rivers and lakes is online. www.canalrivertrust.org.uk

Scotland's canals are looked after by Scottish Canals www.scottish-canals.co.uk

RIGHT: Tardebigge Locks on the
Worcester & Birmingham Canal

Simon Salem,
Marketing Director, Canal & River Trust:

"We know that people feel connected to canals and rivers in a very special way. Keeping people, nature and history connected is what the Canal & River Trust is here to do and we think that the logo embodies that superbly. In 200 years' time I hope that the logo will be as close to the nation's heart as canals are today."

Regional Index - at a glance

Index

ABOVE: Navvy boy with donkeys near Corbett's Bridge on the Montgomery Canal